SMART WOMEN, SMART HABITS

Powerful Practices to Create Your Ideal Financial Future

OBU RAMARAJ

Smart Women, Smart Habits
Powerful Practices to Create Your Ideal Financial Future

Copyright © 2020 Obu Ramaraj

Disclaimer

The publisher and the author make no representations or warranties with respect to the accuracy or completeness of the contents of this work and specifically disclaim all warranties, including without limitation warranties of a financial nature. The advice and strategies contained herein may not be suitable for every situation.

Neither the publisher nor the author is engaged in rendering professional advice or services to the individual reader. The ideas and suggestions contained in this book are not intended as a substitute for professional advice. If professional assistance is required, the services of a competent professional should be sought.

Every effort has been made to ensure that this book is free from error or omissions. The intent of the author is only to offer information of a general nature to help you in your quest for an abundant life. However, the author, publisher, editor or their agents or representatives shall not accept responsibility for any loss or inconvenience caused to a person or organization relying on this information.

Images are owned by the author or labeled as free to use from the internet.

National Library of Australia Cataloguing-in-Publication Entry

Author: Ramaraj, Obu
Title: Smart Women, Smart Habits
ISBN: 978-0-9875741-3-8

Cover design by Vijai Mani
Internal design by InHouse Publishing
Printed by Ingram Spark

Dedicated to

My family—Vijai, Rishi, and Raaga—for listening to
all my crazy ideas

My parents and my sister—for always encouraging me

The universe—for always guiding me and
presenting me teachers at different stages of my life

Contents

Introduction. vii

Part 1: Let's Get the Basics Right **1**
Why Smart Women Are Taking Control of Their Money 3
Good Debt vs. Bad Debt 11

Part 2: Ultimate Money- Management Blueprint **17**
Prework 19
Stage 1: The I.D.E.A.L. Method to Shift Your Mindset 33
Stage 2: Create New Habits to Support
         Your New Mindset 61
Stage 3: Set Goals That You Want. 85
Stage 4: How to Achieve Your Goals 113
Stage 5: Persevere and Review Regularly 133

Part 3: Further Considerations **151**
Money and Happiness 153
Couples and Money 165
How to Put It All Together. 171

Acknowledgments. 175
About the Author 177

Introduction

**"It's good to have money and the things that money can buy,
but it's good, too, to check up once in a while and make sure
that you haven't lost the things money can't buy."**

–George Horace Lorimer

Who likes money? I do.

As long as we live on planet Earth and money is the main medium, all of us need money to satisfy our basic needs of food, clothing, and shelter. When we have plenty of money, we get to live comfortably.

So, why are some people super rich, some rich, some lead a comfortable life, and a vast majority struggle? If we look at an overall picture, there are so many factors. Some individuals with little wealth might be in their early career stages, some might have used their wealth to start businesses. Others might have suffered losses in businesses or had personal setbacks or live in parts of the world where it is really hard to accumulate wealth. At the other end of the spectrum, there are individuals who have amassed large wealth through different ways.

But, if you are someone who earns a fairly good income from your work, and still struggle to get by without credit card debt, have you thought, *Why is that the case? Why is it so hard for me to save a portion of my income?* If you are in a well-paid job, I'm sure you are a confident person. I'm sure you interact confidently with people, your friends, and colleagues. Is the struggle only when it comes to taking control of your money?

If this resonates with you, I am sure you have tried, in the past, to remedy this situation. You might have spoken to your friends about how they manage their finances. Or perhaps you attended some wealth-building seminars and webinars, where the speaker went on and on about investing in properties or shares. And yet again, you wondered how you would invest when you were struggling month to month to get by and pay your bills and have enough to buy food.

Every month when the credit card bill arrived, you cringed. Every month, you thought you'd had enough. You just want to get rid of these debts once and for all. But still by the end of the month, you were back to square one.

Sometimes, you look at the woman in your office, the one who seems to have it all and is happy always. You think, *Oh, why can't I be like that woman? What is the secret to her happiness? I would give anything to be in her shoes.*

You know what? You can be like her; you too can be happy. But I tell you, it requires work—sometimes a lot of work from you. But once you lay the foundation, brick by brick, you can get back your confidence, the confidence you were born with. No one can stop you from handling money like a pro—your money, your hard-earned money.

All this requires is a change in your underlying beliefs. The views that were implanted in you from a young age. By whom, you ask? By your parents, when they were talking (or often fighting) about money or the lack of it. By your friends, when you wanted to go out and spend and each had access to more (or less) money. By your grandparents, by society, by anyone who had an input in your life as you were growing.

I grew up in India in a wealthy family and had little involvement in handling money. My parents instilled strong values in me, and I learned some basic concepts about money—always spend less than you earn, don't do/buy things to please others, bargain for a deal (we Indians love bargaining). In those days, in my culture (as it is now in many developing countries), the unimplied belief is that if you study well and get good grades, you will get a good job and earn a lot of money. So, I did just that. Studied well and got really good grades. I never got to work (as in being employed) when I was young (I mean during my school days or after graduation).

Fast forward a few years. I started my own business in Australia, mainly because I couldn't get a job in the field in which I graduated (biotechnology). I became a mortgage broker. During my initial years, when I was learning my trade, I met different kinds of people. Some were super rich (at least in my eyes at that time) and some were immigrants just like me, wanting to set up base in their new home country.

What stayed with me and created the strongest impact from these appointments were women, single women, who were earning quite good money (like $80,000 plus) and still lived from paycheck to paycheck. On the other end, I met some Asian couples, whose combined income was the same as these single women, and they still managed to save a deposit/down payment to buy a house. It used to fascinate me how some people managed money well where others struggled.

In my opinion, there could be two reasons. One is you earn good money but live like a scrooge—you're stingy with money. The second is that you truly understand your needs and wants and make money work for you, not vice versa.

There is a third way of managing money. It's where you understand the power of your mind and use it to bring in wealth.

I refer to wealth here in the true sense—health, money, and wisdom.

You see, in my own journey, I struggled with this concept. I am a scientist in my pre-finance life. So, everything needed to be proven before I would accept it as true. I struggled mentally to "feel" rich in those early years when my business was just growing. Three years into my business, I was introduced to the concept of self-development (positive thinking and the power of the mind). I started listening to talks and read self-help books like *Think and Grow Rich* by Napoleon Hill. It was still a bit beyond my mental capacity at that time, and I couldn't fully grasp the concepts.

My family was (and still is) spiritual. I grew up that way too. But I couldn't understand certain concepts, like why do we have to go through tough times when we are spiritual? Would things not automatically happen if we were spiritual and praying regularly? Would God not take care of it? So many questions and no answers.

It was at this time I realized that practices like meditation and setting goals were actually small steps that my brain could make sense of. It slowly changed my life. Since then, I've come a long way in using the power of mind to achieve goals and also attract. Reading books like *The Secret* by Rhonda Byrne, learning about the law of attraction, and manifesting became my fascination.

What I present in this book is no secret. These are simple, yet effective steps and habits that helped me slowly, yet steadily change my life to what I wanted. I also share stories of women who have gone through hardships, just like you and me. And how they got past it all and are living the life of their dreams.

If you are open to assessing your current life, to understanding what works for you and what doesn't, that is the first step. Then make those miniscule changes, day after day, week after week.

Ultimately, you will find a new version of you. Just like a butterfly emerges from the cocoon, you too will find that beautiful version of yourself.

But be aware, this is not a quick fix—not a do-it-once kind of a book. As with anything in life, this requires persistence and the willingness to keep doing things, even when you don't feel like it. Because that is the only way that will help you achieve anything you want.

Come on this journey with me. I'll show you how you can live the best version of your life. I invite you to try new experiments to help you change how you think, take on new habits that will serve you, and ultimately create your dream life along with financial freedom. Your life will change beyond your wildest imagination.

PART 1

LET'S GET THE BASICS RIGHT

Why Smart Women Are Taking Control of Their Money

"Never spend your money before you have earned it."

– Thomas Jefferson

Long before money came into existence, the bartering system was used. In this model, surplus goods were exchanged for something else that people wanted. Slowly, money became the medium of exchange and over the last two hundred years or so, it has existed as the main source of exchange all over the world.

My fascination to have some savings arose from the time when I arrived in Australia. I realized unless some money was put aside, I couldn't enjoy my life–like eating out at restaurants, shopping for fun, treating my children to ice cream, having money for emergencies, buying presents, traveling, and so on. When my spouse and I were on a single income, and being first generation in Australia, all these things were hard, because we were trying to set ourselves up from ground zero. I did not like credit cards and wanted to live within our means–even though I couldn't live my preferred lifestyle. There were times when I

used to go to playgroups with my son. Afterwards, most mothers used to go to cafes for coffee, and I would go back home because I did not have money to spend.

Throughout history, it can be seen that certain tribes of people around the world were really good at savings–the Indians, the Chinese, the Europeans. They had a culture where they saved money before they spent it. A piggy bank was one of the first ways of savings. In the Middle Ages, a pygg, an orange-colored clay pot, was used by the Europeans to save money. Over the next two hundred to three hundred years, pygg became piggy bank.

The Europeans were not the only people making piggy banks. In the fourteenth century, Indonesians made one of the first true piggy banks–terracotta piggy banks with a hole in the top to deposit coins.

The animal depicted is not a pig but actually a Javanese celeng, a small wild boar. There is also a theory that this Indonesian version was shipped to Europe, but it's not clear if this is true. In Great Britain, an unbroken Majapahit (Indonesian) terracotta piggy bank was sold for a few thousand pounds!

Today piggy banks have become an enduring icon of savings and young kids all over the world use these piggy banks as one of their first method of savings.

Another culture that has a deep-rooted love and a long history of savings is the Germans. In 2018, a small exhibition opened in the German Historical Museum in Berlin. The first savings bank opened in 1778 in Hamburg. By 1836, there were more than three hundred of these savings banks operating in the then German Confederation, allowing Germans to save their hard-earned income for some interest.

One or two generations ago, in India, people used to buy properties with money saved from income. When weddings happened, parents bore the cost from money saved for that purpose. And travel was always with money saved. Maybe the concept of loans for these purposes was not common then. Times have changed and loans are quite common, as the country is catching up with the Western world as economies are changing.

But if you think about it, why did these cultures focus so much on savings? Why not just borrow money, like is common nowadays, and pay off the loan over a lifetime? Think about it for a minute. I did mention the possibility that loans might not have been common. Or, it could have been a cultural nuance that was passed from one generation to another.

The number one benefit of going through this process, even though people might have sacrificed to get their savings up for a particular project (wedding, house, travel), was that once the project was done, they were debt free. See, how smart they were! They lived within their means and realized that being debt free gave them much more freedom than being tied to debt.

Over time, banks got smart and started offering credit products like home loans, car loans, student loans, credit cards, and a suite of other credit products. A credit card is one of the worst ideas that could have been introduced for consumers. Banks forced people (and still do, through clever marketing) to keep spending more than what they earned. In trying to keep up with the Joneses, people all over the world started living beyond their means and putting themselves under financial stress. Using the equity in their houses to increase spending, taking on more credit card debt, buying new shiny cars requiring motor vehicle loans, and the list of temptations can be endless.

Don't get me wrong, I believe when used correctly, these credit products can help manage and also build wealth. But the problem arises when the vast majority of people struggle without proper knowledge and take on more debt than they can handle, which forces them into a place of despair and stress.

A few hundred years ago, women were mostly homemakers and did not earn an income. Husbands were the main breadwinners, and they gave their wives a small amount of their income to run the family. Being the positive kind of person I am, let me assume that the vast majority of women made that small amount work for them, month after month. They had money to buy food, pay bills, and sometimes even save some of it, so they could indulge their children and themselves every now and then.

Times have changed and many women are now working and earning an income. Many parents want to teach the meaning of hard work and encourage children to take on paid jobs in their teen years. Even though their income might not be high, it can amount to pocket money to spend with friends while parents still take care of the major expenses. Some families are affluent and indulge their children, while some parents cannot afford to do that. Other parents want to teach their children the power of not buying all that they want, known as delayed gratification.

But if children feel lack while growing up and later get a well-paid job, can you imagine what might happen? They think they have the freedom to live life according to their wishes. Add on new peer pressures and the demand to live up to society. Naturally, it makes adults take on credit products without the ability to know how to handle their money.

Many young Millennials now feel that "life is short" and they want to make the most of their time NOW—they want to live in the moment. I agree that we all need to live in the moment. But what exactly does this look like, and what if you fail to plan for your future? Let me paint the picture for you.

Let's assume you are a young woman in your early twenties, maybe single, and have recently commenced full-time work, or you've been working for a few years after completing your education. Your main aim in life now is to work, earn good money and enjoy life. If you have no inclination to think about the future, then your fun can look like spending money on cups of coffee, lunch/dinner outside, weekends spent partying or exploring new places, or spending money on clothes and accessories.

As time passes, you find that your spending is more than what you earn. Unfortunately, you feel stuck now and cannot say no to your friends. So, you take on a credit card or two to keep up with the company. And through all this, you need a new car. You now get a new car loan.

None of your friends are thinking about their thirties and beyond, so you think, *I'm still young. Let me live in the moment and experience life. The future is so far away, why think about it and worry?* So, you live from paycheck to paycheck.

Fast forward ten years or so; you are now in your early thirties. You see some of your friends in relationships, some purchasing properties, and panic sets in (peer pressure again?—in this case it might be good). You think, *Maybe I should also think about buying a house.* After much thought, you decide that it sounds like a good idea. By this time, you've been in a good job, earning a fairly good income—so you think there shouldn't be an issue in buying your first property. You do some research and talk to a professional about buying a home. Depending on which country you are in and the lending environment, you are advised that you need at least some contribution from your side to purchase this property.

A little disappointed, you are now advised to save some money before you can go ahead. You are also advised that you can do this if you can reduce your spending. After a chat, you feel energetic, knowing that you can make this happen. Now, how hard can it be to spend less and save some money? After all, you are single and often you've thought about cutting down on your expenses.

The first weekend comes, and your friends invite you for a night out. In your mind, you replay the conversation about buying your first house. You know that not going out tonight could probably increase your savings. But then, there is the other part of your mind saying, "What is the big deal about buying a house?" Your friends are more important and what's life without a little bit of fun anyway? Somehow being convinced that going out is the best idea, you just go.

Time just flies. Another year goes by, and you have not increased your savings by that much. You panic and decide that this year is the year you will make a better effort.

Years go by; you are married and have a family. Between your partner and you, you have done really well. You've bought a family home, your two children are growing up, and over the two maternity leaves, you took a break to care for your children. Somehow you made it work with one income. As a woman, this is the first setback to your reduced income from a pension when you retire.

As your children grew, you didn't want to go back to full-time work. On and off, you've still been working. Whenever you worked, you got a pension for retirement income, which is not as much as what your partner would have accumulated.

Life goes on, and now both you and your partner are nearing retirement. All of a sudden, you realize your mortgage has not gone down because you kept remortgaging your house for various expenses that life threw at you; you have little or no savings; and, on top of all this, your pension balance looks measly, and it won't last you for five years!

How does this situation look to you?

No one, I repeat *no one*, wants to be in such a situation. If you live in the Western world with good healthcare, it is expected that you are going to live up to eighty or more years. Living in the moment is as important as planning for your future.

To be honest, there is never going to be enough money to save. A salary increase will never prompt you to save more. Young children finishing school will not help you save more. Paying off your mortgage will not be the reason you will save more. A wealthier client will not make you save more. Or even getting older will not enable you to save more. All these are excuses for not saving today. Saving money is a habit that needs to be cultivated—regardless of how much your pay is. It is a habit that needs to be practiced over and over again, so it becomes ingrained in you, becomes a part of you.

Our society is a spending culture rather than a saving culture. As your income increases, there is a natural tendency to increase your spending—maybe on entertainment or travel or any other thing that your heart desires. There is nothing wrong with that—as long as you also save and invest for a healthy financial future. Because in this world, given the number of inventions in technology and the abundance of things you can buy, you will always have enough temptations.

For you to invest in anything, be it property or shares or any kind of investment, you will need initial cash. Where does that come from? Of course, from saving a portion of your income, unless you have parents who can help you out! Which, by the way, is not common. Besides, saving from your hard-earned money and building wealth is a game that brings satisfaction like none other!

I want to challenge the way you think, feel, and act about your money, so you can become what you always were meant to be—happy. Explore the way you look at money and how you relate to it. Remove false beliefs and understand that money is only what goes on in your mind. Money is a powerful tool, which used correctly can help you create and experience your best life.

Good Debt vs. Bad Debt

**"Too many people spend money they earned,
to buy things they don't want,
to impress people they don't like."**

–Will Rogers

There was once a hen named Clarissa. She wanted to be the prettiest chicken in town. She had no money, but just a body that could lay eggs. One day she met another chicken, Sanga, who had beautiful pink feathers. Clarissa realized that her own brown feathers were in tatters and no longer looked good. She decided that she'd had enough with her brown feathers. She wanted to look beautiful and decided to get pink feathers like Sanga.

Clarissa asked Sanga where she got her feathers painted.

Sanga said, "Over there, where the three boys are."

Clarissa went to where the three boys were.

The first boy had a cup of pink ink and said, "Give me an egg, and I will paint one row of pink feathers."

The second boy had nothing and said, "Give me an egg, and I will tell you my idea."

The third boy had a big can of pink ink and said, "Give me an egg, and I will paint ten rows of your feathers pink."

Clarissa ran the options in her head. Her mind said, "The first one's too expensive, I can't afford it. The second one's too cheap, something is fishy. The third one seems the best option." So, she chose the third.

Clarissa said, "Paint my feathers pink."

The third boy told her it would cost one egg per ten rows of feathers. She had a thousand rows, so, that would be one hundred eggs. On top of that, there was a service charge of one hundred eggs.

"What?" said Clarissa, horrified. "You didn't mention that before; you mean you lied?"

The boy told her it was not a lie; it was a service charge. He said that the other boys charged it too, she could ask them if she wanted.

Clarissa said, "I don't have two hundred eggs now, but I want pink feathers, so tell me how I can get them."

The boy said, "You can get a credit line and pay overtime."

Reluctantly, she agreed and signed in ink. But now in debt, she laid eggs for the boy, for the next two hundred days. She was quite miserable.

The next time she saw Sanga, her feathers were green. Clarissa asked in despair, "How do you afford new colors every time?"

Sanga said, "I waited for a promotion, and the painting job was on sale."

Continuing our discussion from the last chapter, debt for many people is just how life works. A simple definition of debt is money owed. This definition says nothing about debt being good or bad.

In the previous chapter, you saw how certain cultures around the world use savings for big expenses like buying a house, weddings, travel, and so on. Things have become so expensive and getting loans is relatively easier, which is one reason a large percentage of the population has a high percentage of debt.

Even if you can live debt free, there is a smart way of taking on certain debts that will help you make the best use of your hard-earned money. That is where the concept of good debt vs. bad debt comes into play.

Good Debt

Good debt is an investment that will help you grow your wealth and/or generate long-term income. A home loan can be a good debt. If purchased in the right suburb, it is expected that the value of the house will increase in the long term. If you are quite diligent and manage to use offset accounts and the like, you will be able to make the best use of your savings while paying off the mortgage. With the help of a good professional, you can plan and aim to quickly pay off your mortgage.

Another example of good debt is a student loan taken out for a college education. Student loans usually have a low-interest rate. By getting a good education, you increase your knowledge and the opportunity to get a well-paid job. An employee with a college degree from a good university has a good starting point when it comes to jobs.

Car debt is one of those debts that can fall in a gray area between good and bad debts. There are three keys to keeping a good debt rather than a bad debt.

Key 1: Put down as much down payment as you can.
Key 2: Find the lowest interest rate possible.
Key 3: Do not purchase an expensive car just because you can.

Remember a vehicle is a depreciating asset, and if you spend a lot of money on a car, it becomes a bad debt.

If you are a business owner or thinking about starting a business, business loans can fall into the good-debt category, because it helps you conserve your seed cash and the borrowed money helps you grow your business. As long as you borrow money with a plan in place to generate more business or income, then taking out a business loan can count as good debt.

Bad Debt

Bad debt is debt incurred when you buy things whose value doesn't increase over time. This kind of debt doesn't help in building wealth. The perfect example is Clarissa (the hen) getting into debt to get her feathers painted pink.

For humans, credit card debt is the perfect example of bad debt. The cards usually carry high-interest rates when you don't pay the balance in full within the credit term.

Borrowing money to purchase clothes, jewelry, and items like that is a big no-no! Similarly, it is not good to borrow money to travel. It is really a luxury, a want, rather than a need. Save money to buy clothes and other nonessential items and even for travel. More on this in later chapters.

Another example of bad debt is the kind of loan called payday loans or cash loans. These are the worst kind of loans you can get. From as little as $500 to larger amounts of $50,000, these loans are advanced quickly, and the reasons can range from wanting to buy groceries to paying rent to purchasing cars to emergencies. These types of loans charge a hefty establishment fee and the interest rate is astronomical.

There are some important lessons you can learn from Clarissa's hen story.

1. It is important to learn smart buying habits. Compare prices, look for offers and promotions. Do not buy on impulse. Cheapest is not always the best.
2. There are different ways to pay—credit card, debit card, cash, and check. Learn about each way and their pros and cons.
3. Look out for hidden costs—service charges, delivery cost, taxes. They might not be stated upfront.
4. Always spend less than you earn.

Never take on debt for fun projects. You need to save money to have fun. Live by this rule and your life is bound to be less stressful.

PART 2

ULTIMATE MONEY-MANAGEMENT BLUEPRINT

Prework

**"You can't really know where you are going until
you know where you have been."**

–Maya Angelou

No matter how much we want life to remain the same, life is all about change. If you have read this far, I believe that you do want to make some change in your life. But change is something that the human brain resists greatly. As humans, we find comfort in routine, which is good in a way. To keep up constantly with too many changes, our brains use up a lot of energy to process these changes and integrate them into our daily lives. This is one reason why it can be hard when we want to change something in our lives.

There are always some brain hacks that can help you achieve what you want. They do not require a great deal of effort, but they are persistent, small changes.

I believe that if you want to change something, the first step is to look at your current life—your state of mind, what is happening in your life, how much money you are making, your lifestyle—the whole gamut. Then assess which parts you like and which parts need to change.

If you think finance is the biggest lack in your life right now, understand that this can arise from lack in other parts of your life.

The biggest concept you need to remember is that YOU are one person. There are different events happening in your life–study, work, earning money, interacting with people (friends, family, colleagues), spending time, exercise, travel–the single common factor is YOU.

Let's start your prework by doing the first exercise. This is called the "Discovery Exercise." Complete it to the best of your ability. Don't think too much–sometimes the true answer comes to you straightaway. The more you think, the more your mind creates an answer to your liking, which by the way is an exercise that we do later. But, these answers need to be your current reality.

Time

How do you spend your time?

(Break it down into sleep, work, family, ME time, travel, exercise, meditate, cooking—a breakdown of time from when you wake up till you go to bed.)

1 ....
....

2 ....
....

3 ....
....

4 ....
....

5 ....
....

6 ....
....

7 ....
....

8 ....
....

9 ....
....

10 ....
....

Happiness

List ten things that make you happy. It could be things you do or don't do. It could be people or circumstances. It could be when you go shopping or a hobby—anything.

(Think what you were doing, who you were with, what factors made you happy.)

1
....
....

2
....
....

3
....
....

4
....
....

5
....
....

6
....
....

7
....
....

8
....
....

9
....
....

10
....
....

Spending Habits

I often wonder if spending habits are acquired from parents or if they are habits you pick up after you move out of the house.

I believe when it comes to money, it starts at home. What money conversations you grew up listening to and/or how well your parents taught you how to handle money are important factors that decide your current money habits. We will discuss this concept more in a later chapter, but for now let's move on.

The "Spending Exercise" is more focused on the reality of how well you manage your money now, known as "spending habits." I can hear you saying, "I don't want to do this!" Even if it is bad, remember, to change what is not working, you need to face the demon. This one step and the courage behind it is all you need to take the first step in changing your money mindset, so let's get started with the second exercise.

There are two parts for you to complete. The first part is the "Spending Exercise" questions, which help you answer how you spend money. This is more like a feel good or an emotional "where does your money go" exercise. The key is to be honest when you do this current reality check.

Spending Exercise—Current Reality

- How do you fill your space?

  ....
  ....
  ....

- How do you spend your money? (Do you know where every single penny you earn goes?)

  ....
  ....
  ....

- How much savings do you have?

  ....
  ....
  ....

- What is the one thing that you cannot resist when you go shopping (think shoes, handbags)?

  ....
  ....
  ....

- How many times a week do you eat out?

  ....
  ....
  ....

The second part of the "Spending Exercise" is to find out in "concrete numbers" how you spend your money.

How many of you actually have a clear idea on how much you earn vs. how much you spend?

If you want to save money, you will need to understand where your money goes.

Kate is an advocate of knowing her budget. She says it can be hard initially. It took her two whole days to do it the first time. But once you have done it, it then gets easier. She does this annually, and it has made it much easier to know where her money goes.

So, let's dive into this worksheet, which is a "Current Income and Expenses Worksheet."

To get an accurate picture of your past spending, sort through your receipts, credit card statements, online bank statements, and any other financial records you might have. The first time you complete this worksheet, it might take a while longer than it normally would.

But the key is to be thorough and not miss any expenditures. Some common amounts that can be missed include cash spent on coffees or lunches. So, account for as much as you possibly can.

What we are doing right now is just taking stock of your current life. We will cover in detail how to create your ideal budget in a later chapter. See the "How Much Money Do You Actually Need to Live Your Dream Life? Worksheet."

Current Income and Expenses Worksheet

Budget Planner

Income	Week	Fortnight	Month	Quarter	Annual
Your take-home pay					
Your partner's take-home pay					
Bonuses/overtime					
Investments					
Income from savings					
Other benefits					
Total income					
Annual income	x 52	x 26	x 12	x 4	x 1
Total annual income					

Expenses	Week	Fortnight	Month	Quarter	Annual
Financial Commitments					
Rent/mortgage					
Car loan payments					
Donations/charity					
Credit card limit					
Contributions to pension					
Child support payments					
Alimony payments					
Allowance (for children)					
Savings (for a rainy day)					
Other loan payments (interest-free credit card, appliance rentals, student loan payments, investment loans)					
Other (fines, bank fees, other regular payments)					

Budget Planner

Expenses	Week	Fortnight	Month	Quarter	Annual
House					
Government fees or taxes					
Local housing fees					
New furniture/appliances					
Home and contents insurance					
Home maintenance and repairs (painting, electrical, plumbing, garden/yard improvements)					
Utilities					
Electricity					
Gas					
Water					
Internet					
Pay TV/DVD rentals					
Home phone					
Mobile phones					
Education					
Children's school fees					
University or college fees					
Childcare before- and after-school care (subtract government benefit received)					
School uniforms and supplies					
Extracurricular activities (sports, music, dance, etc.)					
Excursions and field trips					

Budget Planner

Expenses	Week	Fortnight	Month	Quarter	Annual
Health					
Health insurance					
Insurance (life, income protection, trauma, and disability)					
Doctors (general and specialists)					
Dentists					
Medicines/pharmacy					
Eye care/glasses					
Veterinarian for pets					
Shopping					
Supermarket					
Fruit/vegetables					
Baby products					
Clothing/shoes					
Cosmetics/toiletries					
Hairdresser/barber					
Gifts					
Transportation					
Car insurance					
Car maintenance					
Car registration/license					
Fuel					
Road tolls/parking fees					
Trains, buses, trams, shuttles, airplanes, scooters					
Other (boat, caravan, motorbike, and bicycle)					

Budget Planner

Expenses	Week	Fortnight	Month	Quarter	Annual
Entertainment					
Holidays					
Bars/clubs/alcohol					
Gym/sporting membership					
Smoking					
Movies/live theatre					
Music events					
Hobbies					
Newspapers/magazines					
Celebrations					
Eating Out					
Restaurants					
Snacks					
Lunches					
Coffee/tea/beverages					
Total expenses					
Annualized	x 52	x 26	x 12	x 4	x 1
Total annual expenses					

Once you've completed this worksheet, you can subtract your annual expenses from your annual income to get your cash flow. If your cash flow is positive, well done. If it is neutral or negative, don't worry. That is what this whole book is about—to reverse that situation.

Next, you can move on to the "Net Worth Worksheet," which will give you an indication of your current net worth. This is a combination of your assets (what you own) and your liabilities (what you owe).

Net Worth Worksheet

Assets (What You Own)	Current Cash Value
Savings accounts Checking accounts Motor vehicles Home contents Personal belongings Pension Retirement money Life insurance–cash value Bonds Mutual funds Stocks Shares Other securities Home Tools of trade Other	
Total Assets	

Liabilities (What You Owe)	Current Balance
Home mortgage	
Other mortgage	
Car loans	
Personal loans Student loans	
Credit card balances Money borrowed Store card balances Revolving credit Other	
Total Liabilities	
Total Assets	
Minus Total Liabilities **Equals Net Worth**	

I commend you for taking the time to complete the prework. It shows that you really want to change something and that you are willing to do what it takes to change your current reality to what your heart desires.

You are already well on your way to taking control of your finances. As you keep reading and doing the exercises, you can refer to the prework and use it to gauge your improvement. See how small changes help you take life to a different level.

Let's keep going on this journey.

Stage 1
The I.D.E.A.L. Method to Shift Your Mindset

"If you realized how powerful your thoughts are, you would
never think a negative thought."

–Anonymous

The human brain is fascinating. Over millions of years, it has evolved to what it is today–a complex three-pound organ with billions of neurons, mainly functioning to coordinate the different functions of the body.

As humans, we take our brains for granted. If you think about it, when a baby is born, the physical and mental functions are limited. As the baby grows, at each stage, new physical and mental functions are learned, like learning to walk, use the toilet, and advanced functions, like social interactions, expressing emotions, and so on. The important point to note is that what you do on autopilot as an adult is what you learned over a period of time (sometimes several years) from when you were young.

If the human brain is complex, your "mind" still needs to be understood. The mind vs. brain debate has been going on for a long time now. Neuroscience researchers say the brain and the mind are the same. By default, a healthy mind is thought to be a mind without any mental illness. Surely there is much more to the mind than this?

In the yogic understanding, there are sixteen dimensions to the mind, which can be grouped into four categories—manas, chitta, ahamkara, and buddhi. The first category, manas, is the everyday conscious mind. It has a huge volume of memory, not just in the brain but throughout the whole body. It manages and oversees the constant flow of sensory information entering the body. In meditation, manas is calmed.

The second category, chitta, is the subconscious mind. Its function is to store and organize all the experiences of manas into samskaras (memories, impressions, and emotional patterns). Chitta constantly accesses the samskara database to provide context, depth, and understanding to our current experience.

Ahamkara, the third category, is the maker of "I"—your sense of identity. A healthy and balanced ahamkara helps you to skillfully meet your needs to survive and grow. Your ahamkara can become distorted by thought patterns and false beliefs, which can lead to pain and suffering.

The fourth category, buddhi, is your intellect. It is the logical dimension of thought, mainly related to the brain, and has the ability to discern, comprehend, and judge. In most of us, the buddhi function is weak and hidden by the activity of manas, chitta, and ahamkara. When purified and strengthened, the buddhi provides a clear reflection of consciousness, improved discrimination, and a deep source of wisdom and knowledge.

This definition of "mind" actually makes sense because we have all heard about the conscious/subconscious mind.

Yogic science also defines "mind" as pure vibrating energy. It is an element that conducts thoughts faster than the speed of light and can create substance from nothing. This is a complex idea, but let's look at an example to explain this concept.

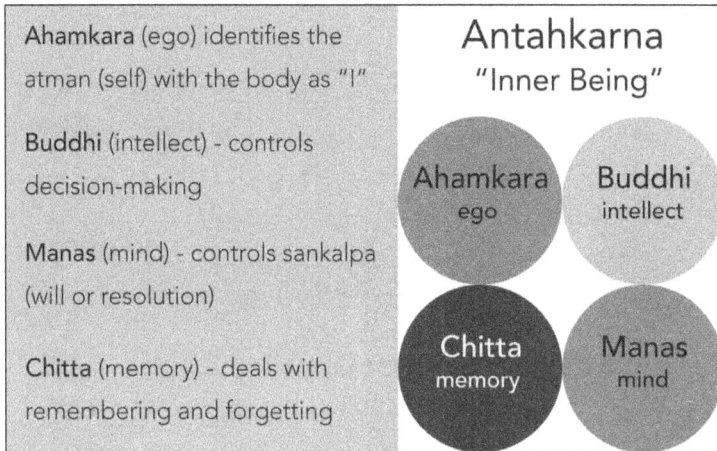

	Antahkarna "Inner Being"
Ahamkara (ego) identifies the atman (self) with the body as "I"	Ahamkara ego
Buddhi (intellect) - controls decision-making	Buddhi intellect
Manas (mind) - controls sankalpa (will or resolution)	Chitta memory
Chitta (memory) - deals with remembering and forgetting	Manas mind

About 80 percent of people who have lost a limb, due to accident or illness, often experience excruciating pain in the amputated limb. This is called "phantom pain." Sometimes, it can be other sensations, like itches, a twitch, or even trying to pick up things as if the limb was actually there.

The sensations of pain are created by the brain. This poses an interesting set of questions. If the brain knows the limb is not there, why would it think the limb is there? Is the mind feeling the limb?

If such complexities exist around the brain and mind, is it then possible to train our minds to achieve what we want? It definitely sounds like it.

I am a strong believer that if the mind can conceive and hold the vision long enough, it will definitely appear in the physical world. For this reason, it is so important to keep your mind at a certain level of positiveness, calmness, strength, and maybe a mix of these at all times. Unless you can do this, any level of action might or might not bring the results you want.

I have created a five-step methodology called the I.D.E.A.L. method that will help you prepare your mind for the level of success—both financially and personally—that you desire.

There are five steps in the I.D.E.A.L. method.

1. Identify your current limiting beliefs.
2. Discover new empowering beliefs.
3. Engage your response-ability.
4. Adopt a growth mindset.
5. Listen to your inner voice.

Step 1: Identify Your Current Limiting Beliefs

Belief is defined as "an acceptance that something exists or is true, with or without proof." Your beliefs, naturally, form your belief system.

The beliefs that affect our lives are either empowering or limiting. Limiting beliefs hold us back from our goals or stop us from enjoying life, while empowering beliefs cause us to reach for our goals and enjoy a greater quality of life.

A limiting belief is a false belief that a person acquires as a result of an incorrect conclusion.

As you grow up, you are constantly bombarded with information and learn a lot both consciously and subconsciously. Most of your childhood is spent at school, where you interact with teachers and also fellow classmates. A large part is also spent with family at home.

As a child, you absorbed a lot of what was going on in your environment. Conscious things, like swear words (of course, we all do); values, like punctuality, respect, honesty, truthfulness, being helpful around home, cleanliness; and subconscious things that your parents and friends did or say. They can be values like how your father treated your mother (respect for women), if your parents encouraged you to express your views (openness), conversations between your parents (life, work, money, stress, joy, parenting), how your friends treated you, the language they used, how your relatives spoke of you—the list can be long.

Many times, the conversations at home could have been about money—especially if money was short. You hear the following ideas.

Don't think that all limiting beliefs were acquired when you were young. You even hear the above statements on TV shows, at school, at workplaces, or even in conversations with yourselves (in your mind). There need not be any judgment on what is or has happened to you in the past. It's important to identify these beliefs, thoughts, and conversations.

Any idea that you accept as true will become true for you, because you act according to your belief system. It is natural for your mind to act according to what you believe, and eventually it appears in your reality.

Let me give you an example. When you were young, did you have a parent or a teacher who believed in you–that you were capable of a task (a project, a race, anything at all)? Assume this person was your favorite, because they always encouraged you and you believed what they said. You wanted to make that teacher/parent proud and put in your best efforts for that particular project. You achieved it too!

There are two things to note here. First, a positive belief from someone you like motivated you to do your best. Second, you too believed that you could do it and you achieved the best outcome.

Lesson 1: Only listen to people who encourage you.

Lesson 2: Believe in yourself.

You might not even be aware of such self-limiting beliefs, but certainly they are there inside. Even if you have made a lot of personal progress working on yourself, but you still find that you are not able to achieve certain things, it means limiting beliefs are holding you back.

For instance, you might, through awareness, say, "I like money, and I want to save money." But, on the other hand, you often end up spending most of it. Or, you might say you love free time but spend eighty hours per week at work. This is sending mixed signals to your mind about what you actually want.

Let's look at some areas where limiting beliefs are common, for instance money. Look at the "Step 1 Worksheet" that asks, "What are your limiting beliefs?" When you look at the word "money," write down the first five words or phrases that pop into your mind. Don't overthink; just write whatever comes to mind– remember there are no right or wrong answers.

When you read each of the topics below, write down any words, phrases, or sentences that come to mind. Avoid overcomplicating this and just do a big brain dump.

Are there any thoughts and emotions that pop into your head? It's okay to be honest, as no one else is going to look at this worksheet. Doing this exercise will help you overcome your limiting beliefs and move on.

Tip: Use the two sentences listed under About Money as an example to find out your limiting beliefs. Do the same for other topics too.

---

1 **About Money**

....

....

....

....

....

....

....

Complete these two sentences to find your beliefs about money.

I'm not financially free, because ....

....

I'd love to have more money, but ....

....

2 About Relationship (With Your Partner)

....
....
....

3 About Success

....
....
....

4 About Health

....
....
....

5 About Work

....
....
....

6 About Me

....
....
....

Do you see a pattern with what you've written? These words are an indication of your current mindset about money. Some of these can be limiting beliefs that are stopping you from creating your ideal life.

If our mind is pure vibrating energy that can bring us whatever we want, doesn't it make sense to think high-energy thoughts that will bring us abundant wealth? We are not taught this at school or at home. If you are still not convinced, here is a story.

When actor Jim Carrey was a struggling young comedian trying to make his way in Los Angeles, he drove his old beat-up Toyota to the top of a hill. This was in 1985, and he was broke. He was sitting there, daydreaming about success. To make himself feel better, Carrey wrote himself a check for ten million dollars, "for acting services rendered," and dated it for Thanksgiving 1995.

He kept that check in his wallet—and every time he was depressed or down, he took out that check and dreamed about his future. The check remained there until it deteriorated but he made the ten million dollars just before Thanksgiving 1995 for the movie *Dumb and Dumber*.

Jim wrote the check, but he also worked hard to make it happen. He took on opportunity after opportunity and did his best.

Now, many people can write a ten-million-dollar check, and it might not appear in their lives. They carry it around like Jim did and look at it every time they are feeling depressed. So, why doesn't it come true for them, like it did for Jim? There are two reasons—one is that the limiting beliefs they hold are not supporting this and the second, and most common, reason is that these people are not working towards it.

By the way, did you notice the time frame that it took for Jim to achieve his goal of ten million dollars—ten years! I'm not saying every goal will take that long, but he was prepared to work for ten years before he could go from broke to super rich.

These kinds of limiting beliefs exist for money and also other areas of your life. The worksheet has other topics for you to complete.

Under About Me, there might be the limiting belief of "I am not intelligent or smart enough," or "I am a pure logical type and can't show my emotions."

On a social level, poor beliefs might exist, like "I am not good with people," or "I am not attractive to the opposite sex." Other general limiting beliefs include "I am too old to do this," or the opposite "I am too young with not enough experience."

And my all-time favorite limiting belief is "I don't have enough time." Every day we put off doing things for a later date. Sometimes, we put away travel until we retire. Sometimes, we ignore family and children until it is too late. And most of the times, our egos get in the way of life. This is exactly why so many couples decide to move away from each other, or businesses suffer.

The concept of "Do what you love and then work becomes play" is catching up quite rapidly. But for the vast majority of the population, work is something they don't look forward to. They do it because they get paid. Over time, they convince themselves that if they don't work hard and don't put in long hours, they will lose their jobs. Is this your limiting belief?

The only truth from the minute we are born on this earth is that we will all die one day. Do you know anyone who is going to live forever on this earth? Some people live to one hundred years and some only live to forty years. But we all pretend as if we are going to live forever.

Even if you can't recognize yourself in these beliefs, there might be other rules, conscious and subconscious beliefs, and thoughts that are holding you back. This is why you need to be aware of your thoughts, the conversations around you, what you choose to believe, and ultimately what you are putting out there.

Take some time to complete the exercises on limiting beliefs for each area of your life.

Step 2: Discover New Empowering Beliefs

If you feel unfulfilled in any aspect of your life, do a reality check about your limiting beliefs. Sometimes, it might not be easy, and you might need help from a professional.

> "The past does not equal the future
> unless you live there."
>
> −Tony Robbins

The above quote means that in a way you are constantly acting as the fortune teller of your own life. If you live by the limiting beliefs formed in the past, conscious or subconscious, you are doomed to repeat the results of the past over and over and thereby reaffirm these unhelpful belief structures.

Here is a real-life story about someone who changed her future.

Christa is an energetic, smart person. I've known her through work when she was appointed as the manager for a bank. Recently, when I was writing this book, I had the opportunity to chat with her regarding her life and how she handles her money.

It was a fascinating story. She grew up with a single parent— her mum—and because of that, they always lived frugally. She learned valuable life lessons about how to live with less and still enjoy life. However, she realized that money was important.

From the age of thirteen, she sold stuff on eBay (this was way before eBay became popular). She used to buy things cheaply and then sell them on eBay for a profit. She created pocket money for herself and did not let her reality stop her. Over the years, through hard work and determination, she created a beautiful, financially abundant future for herself.

It's important to have empowering beliefs, so that you are supporting yourself instead of standing in your own way. As we saw earlier, finding your limiting beliefs is the first step to changing your current reality. Once you have examined your limiting beliefs, you need to replace them with empowering beliefs. For example, if your limiting belief is "I'm just not good with money," your supporting belief can be "I learn and use knowledge about money every day."

In the "Step 2 Worksheet," for each of your limiting beliefs in the "Step 1 Worksheet" (money, relationship, success, health, work, me), write an alternative empowering belief to support you.

Step 2 Worksheet
Expose your own limiting beliefs and replace with positive affirmations.

Limiting belief about money ....

....

Empowering belief about money ....

....

Limiting belief about relationship ....

....

Empowering belief about relationship ....

....

Limiting belief about success ....

....

Empowering belief about success ....

....

Limiting belief about health ....

....

Empowering belief about health ....

....

Limiting belief about work ....

....

Empowering belief about work ....

....

Limiting belief about me ....

....

Empowering belief about me ....

....

Once you identify your limiting beliefs, you then need to install the empowering beliefs in your mind until they become you—the reality of you. How do you do it? I am no expert, but the simplest way that works for me is to constantly keep reminding myself of my empowering beliefs. Repeated reinforcement will become your new belief system.

So, there is conscious thinking and then there is training your subconscious mind.

Do you know what I'm talking about? Remember that time when you got in your car after work and then drove home and then thought, *How did I get home? I don't remember driving at all!* and then you snap out of your thoughts? That is your subconscious mind that helped you drive on the road, navigate traffic, and know the route home—even among the thoughts that kept your conscious mind occupied.

How amazing is your mind? Think back to how it was initially, when you first learned to drive a car. Do you remember how much effort it required? You had to remember to press the correct pedals and also to keep looking into the mirror consciously. Do you think you could have done the subconscious driving then? Absolutely not.

How many years of training did it take—five, maybe ten? But definitely not overnight!

Training yourself to take on empowering beliefs is somewhat the same. It needs to be at a more subconscious level than training the conscious mind. The conscious mind (manas) tends to forget details over time as we fill our brains with new information, but the subconscious mind (chitta) stores the information for a long time and helps us access it when needed.

One easy technique in this age of smartphones is to set reminders. Initially, what I used to do was to set one positive intention for every hour on my phone as a reminder. When it

popped up every hour of the day from
nine a.m. to four p.m. (eight reminders a
day), I took thirty seconds or less to take
a deep breath and enforce that belief to
myself. You can say it out loud (if you're
somewhere you can) or just as a thought
in your mind.

I hear some of you asking, "How long
do I have to do this?" Initially, I did this for
six months. Actually, it's not that long at all. By the way, if you are
looking for a quick fix, this is not going to work. Improving your
thoughts and keeping them at a certain level requires effort!

**Lesson 3: Changing anything long term requires persistence
and effort.**

How long it takes to change your belief system varies for each
person. For some, it might naturally be easy to make those
changes, for others it might be harder. Not because you are not
open, but because it has been a long time since those limiting
beliefs were instilled and you might need to use the help of an
expert (for example, neuro-linguistic programming or NLP) to
help permanently remove these limiting beliefs.

The key is to affirm empowering beliefs from a place of
abundance and not from a place of lack or neediness, because
the feeling of lack doesn't bring the change quickly. But a feeling
of knowing that you are on your path to change, and the gratitude
that arises from it, will help you achieve what you want much
quicker. Once you feel and see the change in your behavior from
your new belief system, you can then incorporate updated belief
systems or keep going with the same.

Step 3: Engage Your Response-ability

"Often we don't even realize who we're meant
to be because we're so busy trying to live out
someone else's ideas. But other people and their
opinions hold no power in defining our destiny."

–Oprah Winfrey

Handling External Environments

Every day in your lives, you face so many people—from family
to friends to work colleagues. When conversations head in the
direction that you like, you are happy. When something is said
that makes you uncomfortable or doesn't meet your expecta-
tions, you experience negative emotions, like anger, stress, and
unhappiness.

In any situation, you have the ability to respond. Look at the
situations below. One or more might apply to you.

Situation 1: If you are in a relationship, at home, between you
and your partner, there are certain tasks that your partner needs
to do, which might not happen regularly (yeah—we all go through
it, don't we?), like the dishes, the laundry, or cooking.

Situation 2: If you have children, you might have times when
they don't listen to you. Common themes might be "How many
times do I have to tell you to finish your veggies?" or "How many
times do I have to tell you to finish your homework before you
can use your device?" or "Can you clean the floor of your room?

Situation 3: Have you ever not wanted to do something but
ended up doing it anyway because you didn't want to say no

to your friends? Maybe you didn't want to go to a pub (because your budget didn't allow or you were saving for something else), but nevertheless went anyway because you didn't want to offend your friends?

Situation 4: Imagine you are driving your car to work; it has been a good morning so far. You managed to get in the car on time and are driving to work. The traffic is slowing and you know you are going to be a little late to work, despite your best efforts to get out of the house on time. To top it all, another car cuts in front of you and you had to slam on your brakes.

How do you respond in situations like these?

Your first response might be anger or stress followed by disappointment or a host of other negative emotions. Do you agree?

In situation 3, if you think about it, you really did not want to do something, but you did it anyway. Why? Is it the need for external validation? Humans are social beings and crave attention.

Life around you will not happen 100 percent the way you want. But life within you should always happen the way you want, because it is in your control. This includes the way you respond to situations around you.

This is not about positive thinking. It is not about denying your situation or how you feel inside. It is about developing resources that will help you deal when situations are hard for you, which sometimes can be really, really hard.

I am not asking you to suppress your emotions. What I am asking of you is far from it. I am a big believer in expressing your emotions. When you are sad, cry your heart out. Similarly, if you are angry, find an appropriate outlet to release it. Use a punching bag or beat the hell out of a wooden stick in your backyard until your anger subsides.

Identify and express your emotion, but don't carry it with you for days, upsetting your internal system.

If it is your child, discipline him or her in whatever way is best. If it is an adult, have a conversation over a cup of coffee and be honest in communicating what you want. At the home front, create rules that help ease your workload (if you are the one doing most of it).

If it is about a relationship (other than your partner), try to avoid getting into upsetting situations as much as possible. If it is your aging parents, think about all the times that they put up with you growing up—be a little more patient as they are going through their second childhood.

If it is a friend who annoys you all the time, break the relationship and find a more positive and supportive friend.

Some things that upset you are also because of the way you were brought up. When your parents grew up, maybe their mothers were not working, which meant they did the laundry every day and kept the house neat and clean every single day. Then demands increased on women—as a working parent, quite often you need to juggle so much in your life, including children, work, relationships, and so on.

Just because you learned from your parents that things need to be a certain way, it doesn't have to be that way. Let me give you an example. If you are a parent, use your children's help with the laundry—from loading the washing machine to folding clothes to putting them away. If you are an obsessive-compulsive person, you might not be happy with the way the children fold laundry, but in the larger scheme of life, if it will free your time to take them to the park, so be it. What is important? Building a strong bond with your children or perfectly folded clothes?

You might say, "Oh, it's easy for you to say that, but my children are not supportive—I keep asking for help, but they never do it."

It also depends on the age of your children. This might sound mean, but how about you don't do their laundry for a week? Will that help?

I am not suggesting that one method will work for everyone. All I am trying to do is to help you take back control of your life and for you to feel that you too are important. Everything is really up to you. When you are faced with any situation in life, ask yourself, "Can I do anything to change this situation?" There is a solution for every problem (especially of the mind).

Handling Internal Environments

How do you handle conversations with yourself? You know what I mean? For example, let's look at your response-ability from a "money" perspective. A lot of women live from paycheck to paycheck because they simply don't understand wants vs. needs.

Their ability to respond to an internal conversation within themselves is quite often leaning towards pleasing others. How so? They feel the need to buy a new dress to show off to the community that they can afford it (when they actually cannot). The shiny new expensive car you bought but didn't need to, that is to show off too. Earlier, we saw how sometimes you end up doing something with your friends, because of peer pressure, even though you don't want to.

Understand or question your ability to respond to your wants. You always need to have an internal dialogue when it comes to spending money. Learn to say "no" to things and people.

It is equally important to find ways to save money. How about buying a used car in a similar model, which will cost you way less than the new car? Cars drop in value by thousands of dollars the minute you drive them out of the showroom.

The aim of this exercise is to understand your deep desires so you can live a life that you want, not to please others.

Step 4: Adopt a Growth Mindset

Difficulty means "not yet," said Carol Dweck. She is known for her work on the mindset psychological trait, including fixed mindset and growth mindset.

In a **fixed mindset,** people believe that their basic qualities, like intelligence or talent, are fixed traits and cannot be changed. They spend their time documenting their intelligence or talent rather than trying to improve it.

In a **growth mindset,** people believe that their most basic abilities can be developed to the next level through learning and practice. To achieve this, the willingness to learn is the starting point. This view creates a love for learning and resilience to achieve great things.

Here's an example that you possibly have experienced in your life. You need to take the 8:03 a.m. train to work, so you can start work at nine a.m. However, you've missed the alarm (because you hit snooze a few times), so you woke up late, didn't do any of your morning rituals, and rushed out of the house without breakfast. You find that you've missed the train and are going to be late to work.

People with a fixed mindset will keep doing the same thing over and over again and get angry and blame themselves. A person with a growth mindset will find ways to solve this simple problem—maybe go to bed early and wake up earlier?

Here's another example. The first part might feel true for some of you.

A woman joined a new job. She was so excited about it that she used to jump out of bed every day, eager to go to work. She was doing an awesome job and smashing her targets at work. But the harder she worked, the more her supervisors kept complaining about what needed to be improved.

She was all for constructive feedback and wanted to improve herself. But she wanted some appreciation for her efforts too, because it is human tendency to want some praise for a job well done. After all, we all have a deep psychological need to be respected, valued, and appreciated.

As time passed, she got demotivated and did not feel like getting out of bed to go to work. She even thought of quitting her job. But, unwilling to do so, she started researching positive habits. That is when she discovered the concept of a growth mindset.

Stanford psychologist Carol Dweck has found that changing the way we perceive ourselves can dramatically improve our feelings and results.

In particular two beliefs will help: One belief is that we all can learn new things to improve our abilities, and the second belief is to not take it personally.

So, the woman adopted this new growth mindset and looked at the criticism in a different way. Whenever she heard a critical remark, she would clarify with her supervisors—"So that I am understanding you clearly, can you tell me what percentage of our approach is actually working?" You'll laugh, but nearly every single time the answer was that more than 70 percent of what they were doing was great. Then she asked herself what she was losing sleep about.

What this lady did was reframe a situation. Reframing is a great tool when you find yourself dejected. She turned around a situation of despair to a situation of hope for herself.

If you're suffering from a fixed mindset, and the fear of failure is stressing you out, you can try to reframe the situation and find out all the good ideas to help you keep moving.

What we need at times like this is resilience. When you go camping, what do you have in your backpack? In case of emergency, what do you carry in your backpack that can help you? Similarly, when you face difficulties in life, what do you have inside you—happiness, strength, or lessons from the past that can help you deal with this? Are you a kind and caring person who has made friends who can help you? These are the mindsets that can help you get through tough situations.

Exercise

Think about a tough situation that you are going through in your life right now—maybe at work or in your personal life. How can you reframe this situation using a growth mindset? Are there any previous life lessons that can help you get through this situation, or can you call on your trusted network to help you get through this?

Step 5: Listen to Your Inner Voice

What does your mental talk involve? I bet sometimes you are not even aware of it. Can I ask you to observe this for a minute? Mental talk is the voice inside your head that starts from the moment you wake up in the morning, accompanies you through the day, and stays with you at night; sometimes it is so bad that it doesn't even let you sleep.

You know what I'm talking about? The voice that goes, "Damn, there's the alarm. I don't want to wake up; let me sleep for another five minutes" or "Sam was supposed to send me some information for the report yesterday and he still hasn't; the report is due today" or "I bet public transportation doesn't operate on time today, and I'm going to be late; I should probably take the taxi, but the traffic is bad too."

Do you recognize these constant negative thoughts? That is your mental talk. You pretend to ignore it and sometimes, it becomes a habit. A part of you doesn't even recognize what this voice is telling you. It is like an unwelcome friend who you cannot be rude to; but, whatever you try, it still hangs around you.

In all honesty, this voice is going to stay with you throughout your life until your last breath. It is like an untrained puppy. When you first bring home a puppy, you have to train it and teach it the ways of how life works in your house. Eventually, once trained, it listens to your commands. Life is good for all parties involved. Similarly, you need to pay attention to what your mental talk is and train it to suit your needs, not vice versa.

Exercise

Sit comfortably in a chair, with your spine straight. Close your eyes. Take a few deep breaths to bring your attention to the now. Do not think about your day or your to-do list and how far behind you are. Don't think about social media or what you are having for lunch/dinner. Don't think about the trip you want to take sometime soon. Don't do any of these things. Just sit and observe your mental talk. Many times, you will beat yourself up. Don't go there. At this point, just observe.

Was it easy or hard for you? What kind of mental talk did you have?

As you approach a challenge, the voice might say, "Are you sure you can do it? Do you have the talent to achieve this?" Women especially have the tendency to self-doubt. Maybe we are wired to be more cautious than men and hence a fixed mentality. Let's imagine that you persist at ignoring this voice and still do the task, and if you fail, the voice returns within seconds to snap at you, "See, I told you, you can't do it! What were you thinking?" Sometimes even when people give constructive criticism, this nasty side of your voice makes you feel inadequate and that you are incapable.

So, the first step is to recognize what your mental talk is every time you face a challenge or criticism. I'm not asking you to listen to this inner voice. If this is your predominant inner voice, you first need to work on changing it to a friendly tone.

Next time, as you approach a new task that you are not familiar with, and you hear that limiting voice stopping you from trying, talk back to it saying, "Right now, I am not sure if I can do it, but I am going to take on the task and ask for help and let help appear at the right time." If the voice says, "What if you will fail?" tell the voice that "There is no failure, only life experiences that I collect as I go along the path of life—some of them pleasant, some not as much, and I learn as I keep trying new things."

In my own experience, this approach has helped me numerous times. I have taken on tasks that were daunting, but I had the courage and the belief that help would appear. And it definitely did, at the right time. Over time, I have become good at trusting the universe and experimenting more. Funny enough, help keeps appearing time after time.

People appear in my life, or people who know people appear, and the path is shown to me. But do you know what this requires? The commitment to try new things and the resilience to keep going at it. Because, believe me when I say, hurdles will definitely be thrown your way. It is the way the universe tests you before it can hand over the sweet result you want.

If you keep conditioning your inner voice to thoughts that will help you, over time you can listen to it. Honestly, I believe that when we were children, we were much better at trying new things without worrying about the results. As we grew older, society conditioned us to be more wary, and sometimes that doesn't help us grow.

Ultimately, your thoughts, your mental talk, or your mind voice becomes the reality in your physical universe. This is why it is important to condition or change your mental talk to support you on your journey on this planet.

If you are finding it hard to start increasing your savings, find out what small things you can cut back on that will help save money. Consider smaller wants, like a cup of coffee. If that nasty voice in your head says "Who are you kidding? Saving money by cutting down on a cup of coffee at work every day?"

Change your mental talk to something positive. Talk back to that voice and say, "By not spending four dollars a day on coffee, five times a week, I will save twenty dollars a week. If I save twenty dollars a week for a whole year, my savings will amount to one thousand and forty dollars. That much money in my pocket is a big achievement for me, as I've never saved that much before. With the money, I can take a vacation without burning a hole in my pocket, or I can even pay off some of the credit card debt I've racked up recently." This kind of conversation will eventually help you achieve much greater things.

By the way, it doesn't have to be a cup of coffee. The idea here is to identify what you really love and keep doing that, while ruthlessly cutting back on all other things. If you say you love all things but your budget doesn't allow it, then make a list of the things you love to spend money on and prioritize in order of what is important to you. Instant gratification will definitely not help you in the long run. So, as you work towards increasing your income, work on cutting back on the lowest priority spending on your list.

Some people call this scarcity mindset, but I assure you it is not. Scarcity mindset is the belief that there will never be enough—be it money, food, things, or anything else—and as a result, your actions come from a place of lack. What I am suggesting here is to help you plan how and where to spend your money, so you can save a portion of it and grow your wealth.

So, let us adopt that growth mindset. Over time, whichever voice you listen to becomes your inner voice. This is the only way to change from a fixed mindset to a growth mindset. Be okay with trying new things.

If you want to start living life on a new level, then you will need to make some crucial mindset shifts. The quality of your relationships, happiness, the money you make, and so many other things really depends on your mindset.

You must protect your mindset against the naysayers and people who want to drag you down. You also have to protect it against bad information and against overload. Watching TV, especially the news, is one of the worst ways to stay positive. Just a few minutes of watching or reading about the news and you will feel that the world is coming to an end. I believe if the news is big and needs to reach you, it definitely will.

Keeping your confidence is huge. So, please, stay on the right path, look to improve yourself, and to help others along the way. You can't go wrong with that.

This might sound like really basic work, but good things happen by doing simple work!

Stage 2
Create New Habits to
Support Your New Mindset

**"You'll never change your life until you
change something you do daily.
The secret of your success is found in your daily routine."**

–John C. Maxwell

One of the greatest lessons I have learned in my life, which has enabled me to live the life I want, is to do certain activities repeatedly until they become habits. Then you no longer have to think, you just do it.

What is the difference between habit and routine?

A habit is an action we often do repeatedly. A routine is a course of action to be followed regularly. The main difference between habit and routine is that the former needs a high degree of intent and conscious action, whereas the latter is a recurrent action without giving much thought.

In simple terms, activities you do day in and day out—that is, routine—eventually become habits. A simple example is the way you start brushing your teeth from one end of the mouth to the other in a particular way without even thinking about it.

Everything you do in your life, from the minute you wake up to the minute you hit the pillow at night, involves routine or habit. So, it is important to create a good routine, which will over time become a habit. These habits will eventually help you develop an abundant mindset when it comes to finance, time, or anything you want in life.

To change habits, you first need to understand your current patterns in life. This is more important than motivation itself.

Look at the "Your Current Lifestyle Worksheet." Answer these two questions on your worksheet–honestly. How does your morning and nighttime look?

How do you start your day?

Write what happens from the time your alarm rings until you are ready to go to work.

....

....

....

....

....

....

....

....

....

....

....

....

....

....

....

....

....

....

How do you end your day?

Write about the last hour before you go to sleep.

....

....

....

....

....

....

....

....

....

....

....

....

....

....

....

....

....

....

Morning Routine

All of us have a pattern when we wake each morning. Are you the kind of person who jumps out of bed when your alarm rings, ready to face the day? Or are you the kind who hits the snooze button repeatedly and gets to work late most days?

We all sleep so that our bodies can rest and feel refreshed to face another great day in our lives. However, most people wake up feeling stressed and unhappy about the day to come. Even though they have food to eat, basic necessities, family, and friends, they still panic and feel stressed all the time. Stress and panic were meant to be alarm systems. However, this has now become the norm.

Whatever your lifestyle is, don't despair. Being conscious is the first step; this will help you make changes that will transform your life. Your current patterns in life have been created sub-consciously. Unless, you have taken some effort to design it by intent, like exercise and eating healthy. These habits might have been instilled when you were younger–by parents, at schools, or part of growing up. Most other activities you do have become a habit, and you just do it day in and day out, without giving it much thought.

Growing up has its benefits and also a downside. When you were at school and your parents took care of you, you had healthy food served and you had your basic necessities taken care of. Even though you might have had to contribute, we can all agree that the majority of it was taken care of for us.

Then, one day you grow up. You now have to go to work every day. And you have to cook your own food, exercise to stay healthy, do the dishes and laundry, entertain friends, and keep doing all of this while trying to maintain balance. Phew! Being an adult can be hard. But you can make it easy for yourself.

How you start your day can have a profound effect on how your day unfolds for you.

Let me give you an example of how my day starts.

My alarm usually goes off at 6:30 a.m. I take the next fifteen minutes to freshen up. Between six forty-five and seven fifteen, I usually do my meditation, journaling, and basic stretches. From then till eight thirty in the morning, I get ready for work, get my kids ready for school, have breakfast, pack their lunches, and send them off. By nine a.m., I am ready at my desk to start work.

I don't have to travel to work every day and have the freedom to work around school drop off/pick up. Some of you might have to include travel time of up to an hour, so your morning can be different.

When the alarm rings, I turn it off and lie there in my bed for a minute or two–thanking the universe for a good night's sleep. I then get out of bed to go through my routine before I even interact with others in my household. What this does to my mind is amazing. I will not check emails or social media until later in the day. This means I am starting my day giving my body and mind what they deserve.

Why do I start my day this way? If I check my emails, there could possibly be something that can take over my thinking, and I already start worrying how my day is going to pan out. This then sets the tone for my day, and I don't want it to be like that. Let's not even get into checking social media. It is just a black hole we can get sucked in to for hours–isn't it true? When I follow my morning routine, I dictate how my mind and body feel when I start work.

A few years ago, my routine was different. I used to exercise first thing in the morning. So, I used to wake up at five a.m. for a 5:30 a.m. yoga class. Once I came back, I used to journal and meditate before I did anything else. If my situation changes in the future (which is possible, as work and family commitments change) and I have to wake up early, that is what I will do, rather than give up my morning routine.

Many times (I have been human too), I have slacked off, either not journaling, not meditating, or not exercising, and I can tell you my body and mind have suffered. My day was not as effective as it would have been, had I gone through my normal morning routine.

Life, for each one of us, should happen by intent, not let it go however we feel. Time is what you create for yourself based on your priorities. At this stage in your life, with what little time you have, create a morning routine for yourself.

What can you include in your morning routine? Here are some of the activities I include in my routine.

1. Meditation
2. Journaling
3. Visualization
4. Exercise
5. Breakfast

1. Meditation

When it comes to meditation, even five minutes can help channel your energy and increase focus through the day. There are different kinds of meditation. Some yogis sit cross-legged in deep meditation for hours. Few of us can do that; our minds wander a lot.

There are many guided meditations—some with music only, some with a guided voice, some for health, some for manifestation and abundance. With so many options, you can certainly find one meditation that suits your style.

When I was young, growing up in India, I heard about meditation. But it was more the yogi-style where I had to focus and calm my mind. I can tell you that practice didn't last long for me.

Even through my meditation journey in Australia, I have tried a few different types. Ultimately, I found that I prefer meditations with a voice in the background that I can listen to. It helps me to focus better. Some of those incorporate visualization too.

Over time, meditation becomes easy with practice, and you learn to keep your mind focused. Whatever your style of meditation, this one habit alone can bring enormous changes in your life.

2. Journaling

Sometimes your mind seems preoccupied with one thing or the other, and you just can't focus—especially when your to-do list is long. One of the best ways to get your mind cleared is through journaling. It is a sacred practice for your eyes only.

What do you write in your journal? It can range from your top ten things you are grateful for to a big brain dump of all that is on your mind. You can even do this while drinking your morning cup of coffee or tea or do it first thing after you wake up. Don't worry about language or the words you use when you write your thoughts, because no one else is going to read them. When you journal in the morning, it frees your mind for the day and you no longer struggle to remember it all.

When I first started journaling, sometimes I didn't want to do it. Then I would coax myself to at least write three things I was grateful for. By the time I put pen to paper, my mind would start dumping all that was bothering me. Over time, I realized that by doing this one activity, I used to find solutions to anything that was niggling my mind. When you learn to tap into yourself and get good at it, you don't need to look outside for help. You learn to help yourself—from taking care of problems at work to healing your physical body and mind.

If you don't have even five minutes to do this at home, how about taking five minutes before you start work? Once you are at your desk, take out your journal and write for five minutes before you start the workday. This will work wonders, for the same reason as mentioned before—your mind is now free from petty issues. I guarantee you will focus better on your work.

Everything you do in your life is by choice. This is not a magical thing or about motivation. Science shows that every one of us can be the best in the world at something. What determines your happiness is what you do every day. It is not hard who you were or who your parents were or what your environment is/was.

Here's another example. Assume you need to start work at nine o'clock, and you need to catch the eight a.m. train. That means you need to wake up and perhaps get your children ready for school, pack lunches, and do other activities before you head off to work.

But you might say, "Oh, but you don't know how hard it is—no one helps in my family. I have to do everything, and my children are a handful." As a parent, it is up to you to teach responsibility to your children, to help you, and for them to help themselves when they grow up. Even a simple morning ritual of waking up at 5:30 a.m. and exercising for half an hour should set the right tone to start your day. Or maybe you go for afternoon walks during your lunch break. In that case, wake up early to journal for five minutes before you start your day.

3. Visualization

Visualization is another technique that you can do as a morning routine. Sometimes, you visualize as a part of meditation. At other times, you can do it on its own—visualize your goals (that you will be setting in the coming chapters), or you can visualize your ideal day.

I want to share the power of visualization that helped me in my life. In 2015, it was yet another growth period in my business. As a part of my goal setting, I set an intention to buy our family home. Till then, we had only rented a house. I didn't set a date for this goal but put a beautiful picture of a two-story house on my vision board and as my computer background. I even visualized this as I used to go for walks around my neighborhood. I still had no idea where we would buy or when this would happen. In February 2016, through the powers of the universe, my visualization was coming true. We were gently nudged towards thinking about buying our family home. We started doing the rounds and due diligence.

After five weeks of looking at houses, we were getting a little tired. On a particularly hot day, there were three properties open for inspection. The first one we went to, there were sixteen people wanting to buy that house. From the minute we walked through the house, we loved the feel of it. The backyard was so beautiful. The owners had originally not had any idea of selling the property and had spent time and energy painting the house and doing the garden. Life had changed for them, and they chose to sell. We finished the inspection, spoke to the real estate agent, and said we would get back to him soon.

Afterwards, we had a look at two other houses and liked one of them. But the first house was the best of all. Now, what was the chance that we would be the lucky ones among the sixteen others who came through the door? One in sixteen, I hear you say. Lucky for us, the power of visualization came true, and we were the lucky buyers that day! To this day, I pinch myself when I come to think of how lucky I am to have all these tools (routines and habits) in my pocket.

Visualizing your ideal day (one to two minutes) can be of great help in creating the day just as you would like it to be. Close your eyes and start painting a perfect picture, in the order of everything that is going to happen after you open your eyes–from eating breakfast, to catching public transport on time, to reaching your office on time, to all your meetings going as you wish, to leaving work on time, to spending your evening in a relaxing manner, to winding up your day in an ideal manner, and having a good night's sleep. Many times, visualization can make your day happen exactly how you want it. It might sound weird, but it is true.

4. Exercise

The next morning ritual is exercise. As you know, it is important to keep the body functioning at its best. So, take some time in the morning or throughout the day to give your body the movement it deserves. If not in the morning, schedule at least twenty to thirty minutes of movement every single day.

5. Breakfast

Last, but not the least, is breakfast. Some of you might think eating a morning meal is not actually that important. After seven to eight hours of no food during the night, your body needs a fuel boost in the morning. The right nutrients are so essential for your body to have enough energy to function properly. If you find yourself feeling tired all the time, try making nutrition a priority and eat regularly in small portions. But never miss a meal for lack of time.

There are so many healthy breakfast varieties, from cereals to juices to smoothies. You don't even need to have the same breakfast every day.

Summary

Your morning routine is important. Do not make any excuses, and please don't be overwhelmed to complete these tasks. They might sound like a lot to do and you might think, *not another list of to-dos*. Believe me when I say this—ten to thirty minutes of how you start your day sets your mind for the whole day. Eventually, it leads to other amazing results, like attracting the right jobs and the right people into your life, and even more money! It is up to you to try it for yourself.

Complete the "Create Your New Lifestyle Worksheet." Take some time to complete the first question on how you want to start your ideal day.

Create Your New Lifestyle Worksheet

"Success lies in a masterful consistency around the
fundamentals."

—Robin Sharma

How do you want to start your ideal day?

Write what you want for yourself and what is possible at this stage
of your life—considering family, work, and other activities in your
life; but don't be lazy.

....

....

....

....

....

....

....

....

....

....

....

....

....

....

Remember, nothing is right or wrong. It all depends on how much time you have in the morning, considering your start time at work, your family, and other activities happening in your life. The key here is to be kind to yourself, but not lazy. Choose one habit that you loved in the past but have forgotten due to family or work demands. Try to do that consistently for a month.

Night Routine

Similar to a morning routine, it is important to have a night routine. If you are a parent, you know that children have a bedtime routine—dinner, bath, and a story—before they go to sleep. As adults, we too need a simple routine to help us enjoy a good night's sleep.

Sleep is one of the most underrated rest techniques ever. It has become the norm to sleep less and work more. But, in reality, a good night's sleep of six to eight hours will make you more productive.

Sleep is when your brain scans your body for any repairs needed and does what it needs to do, so you feel fresh the next day. The more you keep going on and on and on, the harder it is for your body to recover. When you don't rest well, you will find that you feel sluggish or you easily get sick.

No two bodies are the same. So, the sleep quota varies from one person to another. You need to find out what your optimal sleep quota is and make sure you get that much rest.

Turn off the TV and electronic devices at least an hour before your bedtime. Read a book or take a shower—anything that will relax your body. Maybe you can listen to some calming music or meditation before you go to sleep. One of my favorite things to do is to write in my gratitude journal the top three things I was grateful for that day. Being grateful (not for the sake of it, but really realizing and feeling in every cell of your body how lucky you are) always brings more of what you are grateful for.

If you are visual person, place a jar next to your bed. Every night, take a piece of paper and write at least one thing you are grateful for. Fold the paper and put it into the jar. At the end of the year, you can see all the things you were grateful for. It will make you smile.

Pick and choose what suits you. Develop a simple night routine for yourself. It is so important to have a night ritual to tell your body—"It is time to sleep." Take some time to write on this worksheet how you want to end your day.

Create Your New Lifestyle Worksheet

How do you want to start your ideal day?

....

....

....

....

....

....

....

....

....

....

....

....

....

....

....

....

....

....

Weekend Routine

This is one of the best parts of your life—who doesn't love weekends? Come Sunday evening, some people even get the Monday blues. Yet you pay so little attention to what happens during the weekend. And the reason you get the Monday blues is because you have not spent your weekend in the best possible way to give your body and mind the rest they deserve.

This is why it is important to have a weekend routine too. Of course, every weekend might not be the same. Maybe the term I need to use is "weekend scheduling." If you are single, your weekends can revolve around friends or your social circle. If you have a family and children, maybe you spend a lot of time taking them to extracurricular classes, catch-ups with friends, or birthday parties.

Meal prepping over the weekend can save time during the week. Make this an important part of your weekend. I discuss this in a later chapter.

Another important thing to do during the weekend is to plan to do nothing. Schedule some time to rest your body. Maybe your work is quite demanding, and you love an afternoon nap—go for it. How about a long bath on a Sunday evening? Just do it! If you do one thing to pamper yourself every weekend, eventually your brain will start looking forward to ME time. Of course, you can mix it up to make ME time interesting.

Complete the worksheet below about how you would like your ideal weekend to be.

How would you like your ideal weekend to be?

Think about meal prepping, personal time, sleep, and social detox.

....

....

....

....

....

....

....

....

....

....

....

....

....

....

....

....

....

Create Non-negotiables in Your Life

If you want to improve your life, the key thing is to have some non-negotiables in your life—there are some activities that cannot be modified.

Time and again, when I hear some of my friends telling me that they don't have enough time to do something, it is because they haven't planned for the "thing" to happen. They are not motivated enough to want it badly. Be it exercise, meditation, taking up a new hobby, or meal prepping over the weekend, create some non-negotiables. In the next chapter, I talk about the eight facets of life. Create non-negotiables for each of these life's components.

For example, you finish work and come home late at seven p.m. Your excuse for not having a night routine or getting enough sleep is that you have to cook dinner for your family after you come home.

Let me challenge you.

What if you take some time to plan and prep meals over the weekend? It will take from three to four hours over the weekend for you to plan, shop, and cook what you need for the next week. But if you do this, come dinner time on a weekday, all you need to prepare is minimal. You hardly need ten or fifteen minutes to prep anything else you need.

This means that you should be able to close the kitchen by 8:30 p.m. You save time cooking, and cleaning up is easy because there are only a few dishes to wash. If you have older children, get them to help you or maybe you have a supportive partner who can help with both prep and getting dinner on the table every day.

Don't you think a few hours on a Saturday or a Sunday spent on preparation and cooking is worth your while to create smoother weekdays? You can use the saved time for relaxation or to spend time with your children.

Regularly allocate dedicated learning time. Have you heard about the amazing TED Talks? There are plenty of inspirational talks from every walk of life. You can spend as little as ten minutes and get inspired. See https://www.ted.com/talks to get started!

It's essential to make some of these non-negotiables in your life. Just like eating is a non-negotiable for most of us to live and function properly, so are these routines important for our minds to function properly.

It is all good to have written down some routines that you want to turn into habits, but if you don't make time to practice, they won't become habits.

Answer the question on the worksheet and write what your non-negotiables are. What is one thing you will do every single day?

What are your non-negotiables?

(Activities that you have to make a priority in your life, but they're currently not; mostly because you are not conscious about your habits.)

....

....

....

....

....

....

....

....

....

....

....

....

....

....

....

....

....

....

Everything comes to understanding what you want in life and how to make it happen, so you can be happy most of the time.

I want to share a story. Once upon a time, there was a woman who was lost in the desert. She was walking for three days without food and water. She was about to collapse, when she saw in the distance what looked like water. "Is it actually water or is it a mirage?" she asked.

With the last bit of strength she could muster, she kept walking towards the water. When she reached the image, she realized that her prayers had been answered. It was a small lake filled with clean, spring-fed water. There was so much water, that it would last her a lifetime—more than she could ever drink. As she stood there watching the water and almost dying of thirst, she couldn't bring herself to drink it.

There was a passerby riding on a camel from a nearby town. He watched the woman's bizarre behavior for some time, and he couldn't understand why the woman was just standing there. He got off his camel, went to the woman, and asked, "Madam, why don't you drink some water to quench your thirst?"

She looked up at the man with an exhausted, distraught face and told him, "There is so much water here. I know I am dying of thirst, but I can't possibly finish all this water." She started crying.

The passerby smiled, bent down, scooped a handful of water, lifted it to the woman's mouth, and said, "Ma'am, your opportunity right now, and as you move throughout the rest of your life, is to understand that you don't have to drink the whole lake to quench your thirst. You can take one sip, a small sip, and then another and another, if you choose. Focus only on the mouthful in front of you, and all your anxiety, fear, and overwhelm will gradually fade."

Don't be overwhelmed like this woman. Just pick one habit—maybe even getting a little bit more sleep—and do it for a week.

See how amazing your body feels. When you experience this "Oh, my gosh, this is amazing" kind of feeling, make sure you soak it up. Let your mind relate the good feeling to the activity. Then give thanks for having been able to experience that. Keep doing this for every new habit you take on, and your brain will find it easier to take on new habits.

These rituals, when done consistently, can help you find the energy and focus needed to lead an optimal life. You will achieve balance mentally, emotionally, physically, and spiritually. This is the foundation for creating a new empowered life.

Lesson 4: Don't live your life by default. Live by design to create the best version of yourself.

Here's a list of thirty good habits that you can choose from to start living your life by design.

1. Take at least one action to move towards your goal.
2. Plan your day.
3. Visualize your perfect day.
4. Reflect on your day.
5. Save money.
6. Exercise.
7. Pursue at least one hobby from your childhood.
8. Eat healthy.
9. Organize your home.
10. Organize your workplace.
11. Wake up early, consistently.
12. Take a power nap.
13. Regularly set new milestones at work.
14. Set short-, medium-, and long-term goals.
15. Drink at least eight glasses of water a day.

16. Meditate.
17. Get enough sleep.
18. Practice a winding-down ritual (nighttime).
19. Have a morning ritual.
20. Make your bed every morning.
21. Do something fun every day.
22. Clear your clutter.
23. Read for at least thirty minutes a day.
24. Watch an inspirational video at least once a week (for example, TED Talks).
25. Write in your gratitude journal every day.
26. Spend time with your family.
27. Perform an act of kindness.
28. Live in the moment.
29. Devote time to your pet project.
30. Spend time with yourself regularly.

Stage 3
Set Goals That You Want

"It is important to have a dream no matter how old you are."

–Yuichiro Miura

How many of you have set goals in the past? How many of you have set goals and been frustrated that you haven't been able to achieve them? (Don't cringe if you have, because all of us, at some point, have been there.)

Quite often a new year comes, you get excited, and you take on new resolutions—eat healthy, exercise more, lose weight, read more books, watch less TV, go on a trip, or save money. Most of you forget your goals by the end of January. Right? Life happens, you get busy with work and routines, tiredness sets in, and the goals are all forgotten until the next new year.

This can be a common occurrence for many people. When this happens, it discourages some people to never set goals, ever again, because it didn't work the first time. They get frustrated and say, "No more goal setting; it is a stupid thing to do. It doesn't actually work for me."

Here Are Seven Common Reasons Why People Don't Set Goals

1. Tried and Failed Before

If you have ever failed at achieving any goal, your brain retains this piece of information so clearly that the next time you even think about setting goals, it sends alarm bells. The brain has already linked "not achieving goals" with negative emotions, like the fear of rejection, embarrassment, failure, and criticism.

As humans, of course, we like familiarity and praise, not embarrassment or criticism. Your brain, therefore, discourages you from setting new challenges and you ultimately lose interest, just like "The Fox and the Grapes," an Aesop's fable. It is a concise story but has a powerful message. The story is about a fox that tries to eat grapes hanging from a vine. The grapes are high, and the fox cannot reach them. Rather than admit defeat, he goes away saying the grapes are sour and that is why he didn't eat them.

Solution: Don't be like the fox. If you've tried and failed, try again, or get some help. Babies are really good at trying. We, as adults, take walking and talking for granted, among a few other things we do on autopilot. If you, as a baby, didn't try, fall, get up, and try again a zillion times learning to walk, you wouldn't be walking today. Think about that for a minute.

When we are younger, we are more open to trying new things—failing and then getting better at it. But as we grow older, our brains restrain us from doing this. This leads us to the next reason we don't set goals.

2. Clarity

The second reason why you might fail at your goals is because you lack clarity. A classic new year goal is to lose weight gained over the holiday season. In most countries, there is some down time during the season for you to rest and rejuvenate. With this comes good food (usually high calories) and it is normal to gain weight.

So, naturally, come the new year, one of your goals is to lose weight. The goal itself is a good one to maintain health, but it is vague. Remember, if you don't know the destination, it is harder to achieve it.

Solution: Let's explore how you can add some clarity to this goal? Define how much weight you want to lose—is it five or seven pounds of body fat? To add more detail, you can say, "I want to lose five pounds over the next three months." This is a clear goal, one that gives you better direction than "wanting to lose weight."

Without clarity, you will be like a car driving around without headlights at night.

3. Want Results Overnight

Are you one of those people who wants everything yesterday? You know the person who is 30 pounds overweight and wants to have that perfect body in one month? Or the individual who earns $75,000 annual income and wants to earn a million dollars the next year?

Many people expect things to happen overnight. Sometimes, they work towards a goal for a few days, expect miracles, and when it doesn't happen, they lose interest in the goal.

Solution: Ask any successful person—be it business, health, or any field—and they will tell you that overnight results are a fad. Anything worthwhile achieving takes a long period of time. It is important to have patience and discipline.

Let's do a fun activity. The next time you meet your parents (or you can call them now), ask them how long it took you to learn to walk when you were a baby and at what age you started walking. Or, for that matter, ask how long it took to potty-train you (yes, I know!). If you are a parent, you know it takes a long time to learn and achieve anything of significant value.

Learn to be patient and consistent in your actions.

4. Expect Results without Action

You know what is a far worse than wanting overnight results? You don't work towards your goals at all and expect your life to change overnight without any action. Just by writing down your goals, do not assume they will somehow suddenly appear in your lives.

No one, I repeat, no one, other than you, has the power to manifest your goals. A big part of that manifestation is taking action—some action, any action. If you don't move even a finger and expect results to appear, well, we don't live in that kind of a magical world.

Lesson 5: Magic happens with action.

Solution: This is why it is important to identify your true wishes before you set goals; goals that will bring joy when you work towards it. As philanthropist and investor Sir Richard Branson says, "My general attitude to life is to enjoy every minute of every day." If you say, "Oh, God, I've got to do this," then it is going to be hard to keep doing it.

5. Don't Know How

This is a big concept. Sometimes, you are passionate and want to achieve your goals at any cost. But you don't have enough knowledge to achieve them. Consider the example of losing weight: if you want to lose the fat around your belly, concentrating on your abs alone might not help. You might need to build core strength and muscle before you start losing weight. A big part of a weight-loss goal includes the right kind of nutrition.

Solution: With a smartphone in your pocket and access to the internet, not knowing how, cannot be an excuse. If you want to lose weight, you can find hundreds of videos on different exercise routines and plenty of websites about nutrition. Make use of knowledge available to you for free, which was probably not an option for your parents. If you struggle trying to do it yourself, seek a professional to help you achieve your goal. For exercise, it might be a personal trainer or a yoga class; for business and work, it might be a mentor.

Don't let lack of knowledge stop you from achieving your goals.

6. Environment

Your environment plays a big role in shaping you in every way. When you were at school, did you have a positive influence or were your surroundings not conducive to explore your full potential? How was your family environment when you grew up? What about your work environment now?

Your mind is a powerful thing beyond your imagination. If you have ever tried setting a goal and failed, your mind can create a movie with so much drama, a film that can possibly win an award. It can create vivid scenes where all the people in your life are making fun of you, the way they talk behind your back, and sometimes you even think they are looking down on you. Most times, this might not have even happened in real life. But if it ever has, not having a supportive environment might limit you from ever again setting goals.

Solution: Even though a part of this comes from not having the right mindset, you can minimize drama by surrounding yourself with people who support you. You are the average of the five people you surround yourself with. Remember that the next time you set goals. As business magnate and investor Warren Buffett said, "It's better to hang out with people better than you." Surround yourself with amazing people who can hold you accountable and also motivate you every time you are struggling.

7. Can't Do vs. Don't Want To

The seventh common reason is "can't do vs. don't want to." You know sometimes you set goals because everyone else is setting similar goals or maybe someone else wanted you to accomplish something. Maybe you wanted to lose weight because everyone around you was doing it or your doctor asked you to do it. Regardless of how much you try, your mind is not into it. If you really don't want to do something, your mind will find a thousand excuses to not do it.

Low desire equals low effort.

On the work front, your goal might be to secure a promotion by the end of the year. It might be an easy goal to visualize. But if you turn up late to work every day and leave early, miss important meetings, and fall behind schedule all the time, do you think you will get that promotion? It just shows that your desire for a promotion is really low and you can't be bothered.

Solution: If you want to achieve a goal, it needs to bother you (in a good way). So, align your goals with desire.

"A goal properly set is halfway reached."

–Zig Ziglar

A miller, his young son, and their donkey were making their way into the market, where the miller intended to sell the donkey. As they passed a house, a neighbor jeered at them. "What fools! See how they walk when they have a perfectly good donkey?"

So, the miller, feeling embarrassed, had his son ride on the donkey. Later, they passed a group of old men. "See," said one of the men, "this goes to my point: the youth today have no respect for their elders. Here a tired old man is forced to walk while his young, lazy son rides at his side."

Again embarrassed, the miller had his son dismount and the miller sat on the donkey's back. Soon enough, they came upon a group of washerwomen. "What a cruel old man!" said one of the women. "Riding so easy, while his little son struggles to keep pace."

So, the miller had his son join him on the donkey, and they rode together into town. There a man hailed them. "What a burden to place on a donkey! That's too much weight. I'd say the pair of you are better suited to carry that donkey than he is to carry the pair of you."

Hearing this, the miller and his son jumped off the donkey and hefted the unhappy beast up on their shoulders. They came to a bridge in the middle of the town. As they crossed, the donkey became upset at the sound of the rushing water. The donkey kicked and bucked and fell out of the grasp of the miller and his son, tumbling down into the water and disappearing. Having nothing to sell, the miller and his son returned home empty-handed.

Moral: In life, you're going to meet a lot of well-intentioned people who think they know what's best for you. They'll question your choices and offer you their opinions of what's best. A lot of times they'll be wrong. Trust in yourself. Pick the path you think works best for you.

Five Questions to Ask Yourself When Setting Goals

If setting goals is a guiding star for your journey, then setting the right goals is even more important because you don't want to travel a long way and then find out that you have been following the wrong star, when you're about to achieve your goal. It is for this reason that it is better that you don't set goals until you know what you exactly want.

Over time, society has trained people to measure success in terms of career and how much money they make. Work has taken over your life and has become a priority till you retire. For some, a wakeup call in the form of life-changing events like disease, accident, or death of a loved one makes them step back and reassess their priorities in life. Why do we need an incident to get us on a path that truly matters to us? Why not, at this point in time, right now, take a breather to sit and assess where you are and where you want to go?

If each one of us can do this, imagine what kind of society we would live in? If you are single and can re-engineer your life consciously, imagine the kind of partner you can attract. If you are a parent and do this, imagine the impact you can have on your children and family. If you are in your forties, fifties, or sixties, it is never too late to set goals that *you* want to achieve.

When I first set goals, many years ago, I too was sucked into setting goals only for my career. I saw other successful people in my field (mostly men) and thought, to be successful, I needed to earn a certain amount of money. So, I set goals to make $$ per month. To do that, I broke down my goals further—meet "x" number of clients and convert "y" number of clients; do this task plus work on my business, network, and on and on. Everything was about my business.

What I did not realize, at that time, was that I, as a person, was not just about my career. I had other aspects of myself that made me a whole person. I was a mother, a wife. I had to take care of my health and that of my family. I had home duties and also had to have some down time to spend by myself and with family and friends.

Over the years, through my own experience, I realized this truth and found facets of life that made me feel like a complete person. I've grouped these into eight categories (something that works for me). My goal setting spans these eight categories and when I set goals this way, I feel fulfilled in my life.

I feel that I'm doing all that my heart desires, not some time in the future, but right now. I feel like I have power and control over my life through the activities I do. I try to live life from a place of all-inclusiveness, rather than a bit here and a bit there, wishing that when I retire, I can focus on aspects other than work.

Here are the eight facets that make my life whole.

- Money and finance (how much I want to make, save, and invest)
- Business/Career (what kind of job/business)
- Relationships (family, friends, acquaintances, and colleagues)
- Health and wellness (fitness, eating habits, mental health)
- Recreation and play (ME time, hobbies)
- Personal and spiritual (meditate, connect with higher source/God/yourself)
- Personal environment (home and work environment)
- Service and contribution (charity work, contribute time to a cause)

If using these eight facets helped me realize what living life fully meant, the five simple, powerful questions below added depth and clarity to the kind of goals I wanted to set. Once you answer these questions, you are going to fast-track achieving your goals.

The first, big question to ask yourself is this.

1. "What do I really want?"

As seen in the story of the miller, his son, and their donkey, the problem with many people when setting goals is that they set goals to please others (workplace, supervisor, family, society). I strongly encourage you to be honest with yourself.

I relate this concept with the analogy of the safety demonstration before flight takeoff–"In case of emergency, put on your oxygen mask first, before you help your child and others." Unless you help yourself first, you might not be of much use to others. Similarly, in life too, self-help needs to be prioritized, so you can help others better. Think about what you want in each of the eight categories.

Clarity leads to power, and power gives you the ability to act. What do you want in each area of your life? The key word here is *"you"*–what is right for you? Not necessarily what your parents wanted or what your friends or family want for you, and definitely not what society or the media says you should want. What do *you* really want your life to be like in your heart and in your soul? It is also about what you want **today**, not ten years or five years or even one year ago.

Remember, you can do this exercise every year to adjust the course of your journey and to set bigger and better goals as you advance in your journey called life.

Let us look at each category and how it can look.

Money and Finance

Most people define "success" based on how much money they earn. In reality, most people struggle to come up with $1,000 for emergencies. And maybe this is why success really means having more money. But even in terms of more money, what does that mean? What does being rich mean to you? Not everyone wants to be a billionaire or even a millionaire.

I want to share a story that will sort of put into context what I am trying to say. Once there was a small coastal town in Europe. A fisherman used to go fishing every day, get a good catch of fish, come back into town, and sell the whole lot before mid-day. He then had lunch with his family and took a siesta (being a tropical country, it's common, you know). In the evening, he would stroll into the village and spend time with his friends before going back home for dinner to spend time with family.

One day, a smart marketing person happened to go into this town and see that the fisherman was successful in what he was doing. Being the marketer he was, he thought he could help this fisherman grow his business. He told the guy, "Let me help you become more successful." When the fisherman asked how, the marketer said if he got a fancy boat and equipment, he could catch more fish, sell all of them, and make more money.

The fisherman asked, "Then what?"

The marketer replied, "You can get more boats, employ more people, catch more fish, export them, make plenty of money, and become a millionaire."

The fisherman again asked, "Then what?"

The marketer replied, "You will be old by then and you can retire in a small fishing town like this!"

See what I mean? Sometimes, we keep aiming for more and more, without stepping back and analyzing what we truly want and what we have in our life now.

Well, maybe you are not in the same boat as the fisherman (pun intended) and truly want something in your life. The key then is to understand what *you* want.

What does rich mean to you? For example, do you want to own five positive cash flow properties in the next ten years? How much money do you want to earn in the next year? What amount of money in a bank account would make you feel comfortable? Usually, the figure is about $30,000 to $50,000. Maybe you want to start by paying off your debts. Or you want to save enough money for your children's education.

Business/Career

Whether you are a business owner or working for someone, this is definitely a big part of your life. So, choose carefully.

If you are running a business, what do you want from business? How much sales do you want to make annually– $150,000, $500,000, or millions? What kind of culture do you want to create? Do you want to increase the revenue by one or ten times? How many employees do you have, and do you want to hire more people?

If you are working for someone, are you happy in your job? Is it time to change careers? What kind of job is your dream job? If you are happy with your current job, do you want to aim for that promotion you've been longing for? What kind of income do you want to make from your job? What skills will help you get there? If you could upskill just for fun, what would you learn?

Maybe you are an entrepreneur but have had enough. You want to wrap it up and go work for someone or vice versa.

Relationships

Quite often, we ignore this category for the sake of making more money. What do you want your personal relationships to look like? Do you want to find a loving partner? What qualities do you want to see in your partner? How do you want to present yourself to your partner? If you are already in a relationship, do you spend enough quality time with each other? How about a monthly date night? How about a fortnightly chat with each other about your dreams? Maybe you want to spend quality time with family every day.

What kind of friends do you want in your life? What qualities do they embody? Can you see them lifting you up when you are down and vice versa? How much time do you want to spend with them? What kinds of activities do you do together? Picture your ideal social life—the people, the places, and the conversations.

How is your relationship with your colleagues at work or with your business partners? What about your supervisors? Is there anything you can do to deepen your work relationships? What do you really want?

Health and Wellness

"Health is wealth" is an often-heard phrase. Sometimes we ignore this for the sake of making more money. How do you want your body to look and feel every day? How about at the end of the year? What kind of exercise regimen are you going to commit to? If you already have an exercise routine, do you want to explore something new, to add some variety? Do you want to train to achieve some goals—maybe run a marathon?

What about your eating habits? Maybe you can aim to eat food consciously and maintain a healthy diet (eat more fruits and veggies), or you might aim to cut out sugar.

How do you want to feel mentally (think sharp, focused, calm)? Do you want to read self-help books (maybe five a year) to challenge and improve your thoughts and belief systems? What habits do you want to take on to make mental health a part of your life?

Recreation and Play

As women, we often put others before thinking about taking care of ourselves. How do you want to spend play time? Do you see yourself taking up a hobby you've always wanted to? How about a painting class, learning a new language, cooking, singing, or photography? What new creative activity can you learn instead of watching TV for hours on end.

How does your weekend look like? Do you make some time to spend by yourself—maybe take long baths with a good book or a glass of wine? What is one thing that you would like to do for yourself but never have the time to?

Have you always wanted to take a holiday by yourself or with girlfriends? Schedule it now!

Personal and Spiritual

Quite often, when we grow up with certain religious beliefs, we stick with them until we discover other beliefs that we can relate to. Or maybe your own religious beliefs are being explained better by someone else. Regardless of your current beliefs or nonbelief, there is definitely a higher power that helps you in your life. Some people call this power God, some call it higher source or spirit, or maybe it is a big ball of positive energy that you can draw on. Whether you are religious or not, you need to connect with yourself (spiritually) on a daily basis to stay grounded.

Where are you now in your spiritual life? Whether you believe in God or a higher source, what are your practices? Is there a new practice you would like to take on—created from your own spiritual life experiences? How would you like to evolve in your spiritual practices? Would you like to learn the law of attraction and manifestation or deeper states of meditation?

Personal Environment

I am a big believer that a clean environment will help your mind function better. Sometimes, my family thinks I am obsessive with cleanliness. But don't take my word, research has found that people who described their home as "cluttered" or "teeming with unfinished projects" were more likely to be fatigued and depressed. In contrast, people who described their home as "restful" and "restorative" had higher levels of happiness and mental well-being. Similarly, a clean, organized work environment can help you feel in charge and be productive.

So, how would you like your home to be? Is it a source of joy to come home to every night after work? Describe your ideal home environment, your favorite room. What do you fill this room with? Describe the smell of the room. Get vivid. Describe your bedroom—is it a beautiful space to retire at the end of the day? Do you have a garden? What beautiful plants grow there? What seeds would you like to plant in the future?

If you want to move to a new home or even a new country, think about it, make some plans.

On the material front, if you are after a new car, be specific about the make, model, and color. This makes it easier for your brain to visualize and make it happen for you.

Now imagine the perfect workspace. Describe where you can do your best work.

Service and Contribution

However hard-pressed you might be for time and/or money, giving back always brings more into your life. This can be towards your friends, family, or society in general. Choose a charity—you can donate ten dollars a month to make a difference to someone else's life and feel gratitude for being able to do so. Or you can choose to donate a few hours of your time every week for some volunteer work.

If you say it is hard to find a place to volunteer, go to your local aged care and spend time there every weekend. Are you able to spend one hour at the soup kitchen? How about volunteering your skills at the local hospital? Would you like to fundraise for a cause that is close to your heart?

And sometimes, being a parent can be your way of service and contributing. Remember, it is not always about money; time matters too. See the joy you spread and the satisfaction you get in return.

How would you like to contribute?

Once you've answered the question, "What do I really want?"' the second question to answer is this.

2. "Why do I want it?"

Your "why" is your biggest motivation, and there needs to be emotion attached to it. Without emotion, there is no energy to make the changes necessary to achieve what you want. There has to be a burning desire within you to make the necessary changes.

Here are some examples for the eight facets to give you an idea.

- **Money and finance**–Why do you want $$ in your bank? So that in an emergency, you can take care of it in a calm manner?
- **Business/Career**–Why do you want a promotion? Maybe you want to be of greater service and contribute to your field. Can your increased income help do charity work? In both cases, you get a feeling of satisfaction.
- **Relationships**–Better relationships with everyone is going to help you be a better version of yourself–you will be happier.
- **Health and wellness**–Health is wealth. Good health makes you feel happier, and it is easier to achieve other goals.

- **Recreation and play**–As the saying goes, "All work and no play makes Jack a dull boy." Down time is important for you to renew and refresh your body, mind, and soul. Play time helps boost your creativity and you end up happier.
- **Personal and spiritual**–Whether you believe in God or a higher power, we all know there is a powerful energy source that is beyond our understanding. Connection with this source helps us feel safe and secure, and that life is enjoyable.
- **Personal environment**–A clean and likeable environment improves our desire to be in that space and ultimately increases our productivity. A beautiful home is a sanctuary that your family can thrive in.
- **Service and contribution**–Regardless of the woes in your life, there must be some blessings that you can count. Giving a part of your money or your time definitely makes you feel better about yourself.

Every time you lose motivation, think about "why" you chose to set this particular goal. If you still can't get back on track, maybe it is time to reassess your goal.

So, really drill down and understand your "why." There is something I learned with drilling into your why. You need to keep asking yourself "Why?" twenty or more times. The initial reasons are often superfluous and only after the tenth answer will your true motives come to the surface.

The third question to ask yourself is this.

3. "Why do I not already have what I want?"

Let's take an example of wanting to save money to take your family on a holiday. Assuming the income you earn can well enable you to save this money, ask yourself, "Why have I not been able to save this money?"

Look at the seven reasons people don't set goals. Are any of those actually limiting you from achieving what you want? Maybe your "why" is not strong enough? Go back to the second question and really drill down your why—make it so strong that your brain will take small steps to make it happen.

The fourth question to ask is this.

4. "What is my strategy or big plan?"

Obviously to get from where you are to where you want to go, you need a new plan—a roadmap. Otherwise, habitually, you will continue with the old plan and you will not achieve your goal and ultimately get frustrated.

We are looking for a specific plan, but not a perfect one. Here are some ideas for you.

Money and Finance

Let's say your goal is to save $30,000 in an emergency account. Identify how much you currently have. If you have to start from scratch, it might take longer, but do not despair. You need to work out how much you can put away each month and be diligent about it. I explain more in the next chapter to help you with this task. See the "Create Tasks for Your Savings Goal Worksheet."

Business/Career

What strategy can you implement to find X number of new clients? If you have a database, maybe you can reach out to more people? Or what do you need to do to get that promotion in the next six months? Can you show initiative in your current project?

Relationships

If your goal in this category is to spend quality time with your children, can you set aside a half hour after dinner every evening? How about one to two hours during the weekend to do a fun activity, like playing board games or exploring the neighborhood?

Catching up with friends is often delayed if you are a parent. Can you schedule a monthly time to grow your friendship?

Often workplaces encourage team-building activities, like room-escape games or treasure hunts for team members to get to know one another. Maybe it is time for one at your office?

Health and Wellness

What kind of exercise are you going to take up–yoga, Pilates, going to the gym? Decide on how many times a week and at what time each day you will exercise. In the past, if you have tried to exercise after work and always ended up on the couch, choose a different time. It might be easier to exercise early in the day and get it done. If you have a gym at your office, maybe choose lunch breaks to exercise. The idea is to set days and times and stick to it. You can even start with two days a week.

If you are someone with no inclination to exercise, how about you start with walking for half an hour every day at least three times a week?

How about meal preparations on the weekend, so you can eat healthy during the week? Committing a day and time (Saturday or Sunday, morning or evening) will make sure you don't schedule anything else during this time. If you can, involve your children and partner and make it a family activity. With most schools offering cooking as part of the extracurricular activities, children are already interested in cooking. You just have to make the effort to involve them.

Recreation and Play

What is one thing that you can do for yourself? Perhaps sign up for a cooking, pottery, or gardening class? Maybe you can choose to commit to a self-care activity, something that doesn't cost money—like a long bath.

If you were athletic when you were young, can you think about joining a sports group for adults? You get the double benefit of exercise and personal time.

How about an afternoon nap during the weekend? I love my afternoon naps on a Saturday. After the week's work, children's classes, and other activities, a quick nap on a Saturday afternoon helps me rejuvenate myself for Saturday night—which sometimes can be a long night with friends. Even otherwise, I feel more energetic after an hour of dozing.

Personal and Spiritual

Choose the kind of spiritual practice you want to take up. If it is meditation, research and find one that suits you. It can take a while to find a meditation practice that suits your style. You can choose a few styles for several days and find what works best for you. Decide when you are going to allocate time—morning or night?

If you are religious, do you want to practice your religion more?

Personal Environment

There are many benefits of a clean environment. If you don't have time to clean your house, can you perhaps outsource it to a cleaner? Do you have unfinished projects around the house? Does your garden need care? How about allocate one hour every weekend as a part of your play time, if you enjoy gardening.

If your workspace is crowded, make sure you allocate half an hour every week to make it clean and tidy.

Having too many things and lots of stuff in your life is hard. There is a Netflix show, "Tidying Up with Marie Kondo," that helps people clear the clutter from their lives. Check it out if you haven't seen it.

Service and Contribution

What activity would you like to do? You can start with a one-off activity, like helping with a cooking activity for the homeless and see where it takes you.

This leads to the fifth question to ask yourself.

5. "What's my first action?"

Once we have a plan, it's time to act. This is where most people don't get off the ground. Below are some tips to give you some ideas.

Money and Finance

How much money can you put away this week? Do you have to cut back on anything?

Business/Career

What is one activity that you can do this week to achieve your target?

Relationships

How can you be present to your children and family today?

Health and Wellness

Sign up for an exercise class and turn up.

Recreation and Play

Take one hour of your life to uplift yourself, and schedule it on your calendar (remember non-negotiables).

Personal and Spiritual

Spend five minutes listening to a meditation.

Personal Environment

Phone a cleaning company to get a quote.

Service and Contribution

Identify and schedule time to help a cause close to your heart.

Action is critical. If you get lazy with your goals, ask yourself how happy you are with your current life? In most cases, the answer will not be 100 percent. Practice delayed gratification and take one baby step at a time.

When you are doing this for the first time, allocate an hour or more to go through this exercise. Ideally, it is good to do this every year. During the December holidays is perfect for you to set goals for the next year. But let it not be in a rush.

One important tip when you set goals is to not be overenthusiastic and set multiple goals in each category. You will find that your brain will get overwhelmed and nothing will get done. Choose only one goal per category, something that you don't have and is not too hard to achieve.

Lesson 6: Discover your vision for your future and take consistent steps to create your ideal life. While doing this, remember to enjoy the journey and not get caught up in the result.

Goal Setting

Remember, "A goal without a plan is just a wish."

GOALS
S pecific
M easurable
A chievable
R ealistic
T ime Based

	What do I really want?	Why do I want it?	Why do I not already have what I want?	What is my strategy or big plan?	What's my first action?
Money and Finance					
Business/ Career					
Relationships					
Health and Wellness					
Recreation and Play					
Personal and Spiritual					
Personal Environment					
Service and Contribution					

Using a Vision Board to Set Goals

There is no right or wrong way to find the best way to note your goals. But it is essential that you note them somewhere—be it paper or computer or a vision board. When it is all in your head, it is human nature to forget.

When I first started goal setting, I was introduced to noting it all in a diary. So, I wrote out my short, medium-, and long-term goals (up to three years). Each morning, I would take out my diary, look at my goals, and visualize all of them.

I wrote my one-year and six-month goals on one page. On a second page, I wrote my monthly and weekly goals. For example, in the health and fitness section, I included how many times a week I would exercise, and I also had meal prepping as a part of the task for the weekend. For you, if it is about saving, then you can set weekly goals, monthly goals, and then check if you are on track at the end of the month.

Then, on a Monday, week one, I looked at my task list for that week and worked on it every single day. By the end of the week, the smaller goal was completed. I kept going this way week after week. At any given time, I used to have one long-term goal (three years), mostly about work, and a few smaller goals, about family and health.

You can also use cue cards to note each of your goals. Use one cue card per goal. When I was trying out cue cards for goal setting, I used to organize them into short-, medium- and long-term goals. Every morning, I used to flip through each cue card while visualizing it.

Over the last few years, I've used a vision board as my preferred method of reminding me of my goals. A vision board is a visual tool that you can use to plot your future life. Images have a way of lodging deeply into your subconscious mind more than just words. (Think about a movie you saw when you were young—one that you can still vividly remember.)

I like to set annual goals and review them at the end of the year. I often take time to reflect on what worked, what didn't, and if it didn't work, why it didn't work. This helps me set course for the next year's goal-setting exercise. Without doing this exercise, it can be insane to keep doing the same thing over and over again without positive results.

I used to set long-term goals for up to three years. I don't do that anymore. As you practice mindfulness and understand that the universe will give you exactly what you need (not always what you want), amazing things keep popping up in your life and you need to be able to adapt to keep changing course, while still aligning to your big goals.

One year is enough time to think far ahead, and it's also not too far ahead in case an exciting opportunity comes your way and you need to slightly change track.

If you set goals for three years in the future and then a year later your track has totally changed, you don't want to confuse your mind or feel that your efforts have been wasted. So, for now, choose to work on your goals for the next year.

Once you have identified one goal in each of the eight categories, you can get ready to create your vision board.

There are five steps to create your vision board.

Step one: Choose a quiet time of the day when you won't have any disturbance. Turn off your phone and get excited, knowing that you can create your ideal life.

Step two: Take a notebook or a blank piece of paper. Imagine it as a blank drawing canvas and think about how *you* have a chance to create your ideal life.

Step three: Use the goal-setting techniques discussed above in detail. Rather than be wishy-washy, be specific. Think one year ahead and what you want to achieve in that timeframe. Then break it down into smaller goals. How will your half year look? How much will you achieve? Then break it down into monthly goals and further to weekly goals.

Step four: Vision boards can be as elaborate or as simple as you like. It is personal in that it is a reflection of what you hold dear—your dreams. Some people use the back of the bedroom door as their vision board. You can choose a simple piece of cardboard or create it on a pinboard. I like to keep my vision boards year after year—to see how far I've come, but I know people who use pinboards or the back of the door and take a photo at the end of the year before setting new goals for the next year.

The next task is to find pictures relating to each of your goals. You can use magazines. If you, like me, don't have magazines, use the power of the internet. Look online for images. If you are good at drawing, you can incorporate your personal sketches on your vision board. Decorate it any way you feel right for you. You can include quotes and positive words.

So, how many pictures should you use per goal? That is entirely up to you. In the area of health, let's say your aim is to maintain a healthy lifestyle; you can have pictures for yoga and healthy food. In the personal category, you might choose to travel to a particular place that year. Choose pictures of that place for your vision board.

Step five: The last step is to leave the vision board in a place where you will see it daily, say your bedroom wall or a study room. If you are using a diary, then make sure you spend at least five minutes every day taking time to visualize your dreams. When you read each goal, imagine and feel the emotions as if you have already achieved that goal. This also acts as a reminder for the actions to be taken that day.

At the end of the week, check your progress and make necessary changes to reach your goals.

If you truly devote yourself to the process and do not worry about achieving your goals, then something magical will happen! Opportunities will arise out of nowhere, and you will be scaling new heights.

I heard from a spiritual person that if you want to grow flowers in your garden, just doing a meditation where you visualize beautiful flowers will not help. You have to think about the soil, manure, water, and sunlight. If you can manage all those correctly, if you act, then flowers will bloom. You don't even need to think about flowers.

Similarly, if you want to achieve financial wealth in your life, doing financial meditation alone will not help. You have to understand your current state, then create goals and a budget. You stick to it, the action part–that is the most important thing– and as long as that happens, financial freedom will automatically come. Sometimes, you need to have the right professionals around you. Just because you desire the results, they will not come. If you only think about financial freedom in your head, then money will happen only in your head, only in your imagination.

The next chapter shows how you can achieve your goals, including goals specifically related to money.

Stage 4
How to Achieve Your Goals

**"A goal is not always meant to be reached;
it often serves simply as something to aim at."**

–Bruce Lee

I find that quite often many of our "not-so-useful" habits stem from being stressed from day-to-day activities. You know what I mean? If you are a working female and also a parent, there is so much to do every single day. From getting your children ready to school to drop-offs to pickups to afterschool classes to dinner, there are more than enough tasks that can feel overwhelming. All this, after a hard day at work. And it is not as if you can get away from these tasks. Can you?

If you are single, you often tend to bury yourself in work. Work demands are often the center point of your life as you try to climb the corporate ladder.

My suggestion is to destress yourself regularly. Here are some simple and easy suggestions for you—these work for me every single time.

1. Eat regularly. Human bodies need fuel in the form of food. Breakfast is one of the most important meals of the day. It is breaking "the fast" from over eleven or twelve hours ago. Give your body the right kind of fuel to start the day with a bang. Never miss this important meal of the day.

Likewise, try to eat regularly. There are so many theories and mine maybe different from yours. In general, a meal or a snack, every three to four hours, will keep you going. Snacks, like a handful of nuts, might sound like a small portion but will give you a lot of good energy to keep you going. Fruits and veggie sticks work the same way.

2. Take a walk. Every day or any time you feel overwhelmed, step away from the task at hand and take a ten-minute walk. This one activity always helps clear your head. Many times, solutions come to you when you are alone and have the time to step away from your work or any confronting situations.

3. Plan ME time. If you want to live your best life ever, value yourself.

As a person, if you don't take care of yourself, how will you take care of everyone around you? Just like on a plane, if there's an emergency, you put on your oxygen mask first before you help others. In real life, you have to give your body and mind that extra attention, so you can keep in tip-top condition and help others around you.

This will definitely help you be in the flow and do activities naturally. ME time can include things like taking a relaxing bath once a week—with a glass of wine—or scheduling regular catch-ups with your close friends over a cup of coffee. Or maybe you just want to head to the library every week without children to ponder on thoughts that you otherwise don't get to do if you are at home.

Whatever "ME time" means to you, take time regularly for yourself to refresh and rejuvenate.

4. Breathe deeply and consciously. Whatever you are doing now, just stop for a second. Close your eyes. Take a deep breath and count up to four. Then release your breath to a count of four. Increase the count if you can. Repeat this five times. Instantly, your heart rate drops, and you find yourself calmer.

5. Outsource tasks. You might have often heard about "your time being valuable." This is so true. If you are a type A personality, it might be hard for you to let anybody else do the task. Sometimes, it could be that you don't have the cash flow to hire professionals.

It might not always be about spending money. Delegating tasks to others in your household also counts. Whichever way you choose, make sure you get all the people in your household to contribute.

Five Ways to Create Habits That Stick

The last few chapters showed how important good habits are, but a struggle for the majority of us is to be consistent. Other than destressing, to achieve your goals it is imperative to create habits that stick. That is the only way to change "for the better" and to get lifelong addictions to good habits that will serve you.

Practice 1: Create baby steps for macro goals.

This is similar to what was discussed in goal setting about making weekly plans for savings. Take the example of saving $5,000 a year. To achieve this, your weekly savings goal is $104. This can be from packing your own lunch (save ten to twelve dollars per day) to cutting down on buying a cup of coffee (four dollars) every day to any other spending over the weekend.

For some of you, this might sound like disrupting your whole life and your daily routine in a massive way. Even if you try to do this, the habit might last only a week or two, after which you will go back to your previous lifestyle.

If you think you will suffer mentally a lot to cut down so much, how about you take a baby step of cutting down just one cup of coffee a week (not even a day)? To make your brain recognize the baby step you are taking, you can put these four dollars in a jar (or in a drawer) on your work desk to remind you of your savings goal.

Research shows that it helps if you know what you are saving for. Instead of labeling the jar as "savings," use the label "savings for a trip to Bali" or "savings to buy presents." This is exactly what Nicola advises. She says, "When you save with an end goal, there is a sense of achievement."

The idea is to know what your sacrifice in the short term is going to help you achieve in the long run—known as delayed gratification. If you have previously not been able to take a holiday or you've struggled with cash over the holiday period, then you know this strategy will definitely motivate you to keep going when you find it hard to make the commitment.

Similarly, if you are struggling to make exercise a part of your life, and you lose motivation quickly, don't sign up for a twelve-month gym membership that you will never use. Rather, aim for a brisk, thirty-minute walk twice a week to start with. That should be relatively easy. If you are working full-time, you can even find a friend or a colleague with similar goals to go for lunchtime walks with you. After a month or two, walk three to four times a week. Once you find a routine, it gets easier. In time, if you start getting bored, find another kind of exercise.

It might seem so small to start with, but remember everything starts with the first step, not the second or third.

Practice 2: Create behavior chains.

A behavior chain is a string of discrete behaviors sometimes combined with rewards for achieving them.

For example, instead of visiting the café once a day or several times a day, have a cue on your desk. It can be a mug that will remind you to make your own coffee from the office coffee machine rather than go out. If you buy more than one cup of coffee a day, slowly make progress into not buying coffee from outside at all. Again, this comes from knowing *your* goals (helps you identify where to cut back) and accepting delayed gratification.

In another example, let's say you are used to purchasing clothes whenever you fancy, or you spend a lot on drinks on a Friday night. As a reward for not doing it, you can now pop the money you would have spent into your savings jar. Every time you create this pattern, your brain will feel rewarded and your savings will grow at a quick pace. And, by the way, even if you buy a bottle of wine to drink at home instead of going out, you are still going to save massively, and you can put the difference in the savings jar.

A savings jar is an effective way to help your brain comprehend goals and rewards. When you can see your savings growing, you are more likely to stick to the habit. For those of you who can be fairly good with savings, use your bank account to transfer money to savings. Even though you can't physically see it, you know it's there!

Practice 3: Eliminate too many options.

For lasting change to occur, you must ultimately change your environment. Human beings cannot cope with too many options to choose from. A simple example is your wardrobe. It is no secret that women can take a long time to choose a piece of clothing. Do you know that top people, like Facebook founder

Mark Zuckerberg, wear the same version of clothes to work daily so they don't need to spend too much time in the morning trying to choose?

I know it is hard for women to wear the same kind of clothing every day, and we don't want to, right? So, how about you take half an hour every Sunday to lay out your clothes for the week and stick with it? It might be hard at first. You might wake up one morning and think, *Well, I don't feel like wearing what I chose over the weekend.* Stop and think for a minute why you feel that way. Is it lack of sleep that makes your mind all mumbly-jumbly, or did you not realize an important work meeting was scheduled for that day? If it is the former, make sure you get enough sleep. If not, learn to coordinate your clothes for the week using your calendar. I'm sure most meetings are scheduled at least a week ahead.

Planning is key. That helps you minimize distractions and save time and money.

If you want to eat healthy, then don't buy junk food for snacking; pack healthy snacks and take them to work. Make it a part of your meal planning and prepping over the weekend.

I have been meal planning and prepping for a few years now. Initially, when I started, it was hard. Because I was the only one planning and prepping. Over time, I got help from my partner. I usually plan the meals for the week, because it comes naturally to me and I can do it quickly. The bonus is that I get to plan what I feel like eating for the week. We also decide who is cooking what. I do this on a Saturday morning or sometimes late Friday night. Shopping is done straight afterwards, and cooking is done on a Sunday. If we know we have a social event on Sunday, then we cook on Saturday.

In some families, it is hard for men to cook. In such cases, men can help with cutting and cleaning. Remember, it is all about teamwork.

Here is how I plan, so you get an idea. I take a piece of paper and make columns for each day of the working week. Because I have schoolchildren, our plan includes lunches for the children, lunches for hubby and me, and dinners for all of us. Sometimes, I add a row for snacks. For you, you might want to add two rows—one for a morning snack and one for an afternoon snack.

	Monday	Tuesday	Wednesday	Thursday	Friday	Saturday
Lunch (kids)						
Lunch (us)						
Snack						
Dinner						

Our menu includes a variety of food, from Indian to Chinese to Mexican to Thai to meat and veggies. I love cooking, and we are open to trying different cuisines. Our lunches are predominantly Indian, because it is easier to pack a lot of different veggies in different curries each week without getting bored. Also, it is easier to make curries over the weekend and steam rice in the morning. I'm not making five curries for the week, rather two or three curries and then alternate them over the week. For dishes like fish and veggies, we buy the fish on the day and only prep the veggies (clean and cut) over the weekend.

This strategy saves me at least thirty to sixty minutes every day of the working week. I use this time to help my children with schoolwork, spend quality time with family, or even enjoy personal time before I call it a day.

If you are single and come home early every night, then your priority might not be cooking meals for your work week over the weekend. You probably have enough time to cook after work. Instead, you can spend time over the weekend with friends. Or if you want to exercise after work every night, then cook over the weekend.

As my children grow older, my routine can change. I might have more time in the evenings (teenagers don't need much time from parents?), so I can cook dinner after work. The idea is to make it easy for yourself based on what is happening in your life at any given time.

Lesson 7: Embrace the power of routine to help you achieve your goals.

Practice 4: Visualize but don't fantasize.

We've already seen that visualization is a fantastic tool to achieve your goals. What the mind can visualize appears in the real world. All inventions were first created inside the mind of the creator before they appeared outside in the world—from airplanes to telephones to even handbags and clothes.

Once you've identified your goals, the idea is to visualize clearly what you want. The idea is to not get obsessed with achieving it. You need to enjoy the process rather than worry about the end result. The universe sends amazing things your way when you do what you need to. So, the journey should be the most enjoyable part of the process.

Here is a quick visualization technique. If you are in the habit of meditating, you can visualize after your meditation or as a part of it. This makes sure your mind is calm. Otherwise, a simple way to calm your mind is to sit in a quiet space and watch your breathing—in and out—for a whole minute. Make your inhalations and exhalations longer while holding your breath for a few seconds after you inhale. For example, breathe in for eight counts, hold for three counts, and then exhale for eight counts. Once you do this for a minute, that will bring your mind to a calm state.

The reason why it is good to visualize in this calm state is that your brain is in the alpha state, the most appropriate state for your visualization or manifestation to be effective. When you are awake and active, your brain is in a beta state. There are two other states–delta and theta, which require deeper states of calmness, but beta is the daydream state, which is easier to achieve.

Once you are there, with your eyes closed, imagine a big screen front of you in the highest resolution. Let your current lifestyle run on the screen like a movie. The movie is about whatever you are not happy with in your life. Now, take a big eraser and erase your current state.

Next, visualize having achieved your goal, in the clearest, colorful image, all this on the screen. The next step is to add emotions to this scene. See how happy you are–people are high-fiving you, celebrating your achievement, and you see it in great detail. Once you are done, express gratitude for this brief visualization of your future. Slowly open your eyes.

Practice 5: Eliminate the obstacles.

All of us are human, and there are chances we will slip away from that terrific new habit we are on the path to acquiring. The idea is to find out the triggers that stop you from being consistent and eliminate them completely. For example, if you have to wake up early to go to the gym, then the idea is to lay out the workout clothes on your bed, so you don't have to look for them in the morning. Or maybe you can even sleep in your gym clothes, so it is easy to wake up and head straight to the workout.

Another example for eating healthy snacks is to prep carrot and celery sticks over the weekend. Have them ready in the fridge to eat when you are hungry, rather than needing to cut them up when you start to get hungry. And stop buying that bag of chips—don't have it at home at all!

Create Tasks Linked to Your Savings Goals

In the last chapter, we saw how you can set specific goals—SMART goals. One of the last questions to ask yourself was about your first action—"What's my first action?"

We now change gears and move on to goals specifically about increasing your savings for various reasons, not limited to paying off debts and investments.

Here I suggest five different tasks that you can consider for your first action. You can choose one or more of these tasks. Or you can complete one task and then move on to another.

Task 1: Basic Budgeting

Refer to the "Budget Planner" worksheet you completed in the prework section. Was there any area you recognized that you could stop spending money or perhaps minimize your spending?

Did you find any unnecessary leaks in your budget? How about those expensive restaurants that have become a part of your life? Do you know how much you can spend on eating out per week? If you are single, maybe thirty dollars per week? What is your restaurant bill (or bills) stacking up to?

If you think all your expenses are needed, then you should do a reality check. If you are someone struggling a lot with cash flow, then you definitely should reevaluate your wants and needs. At this stage, work on decreasing what you spend on wants.

For example, start small. Are you able to save five dollars per week? Do you think this is possible? It's not thousands of dollars, but you can start small. Over a year, this should give you $260 in savings.

Task 2: Create a Pattern

If you think you can't save five dollars, how about saving one dollar for the first week, two dollars for the second week, and so on. This should give you $1,378 in total savings at the end of the year. If you are starting the process in January, start with fifty-two dollars and work back; because come the holidays, you might be struggling to put away more money. This way, the amount you need to put away during the holiday season is less and you can still achieve your goal of saving.

Task 3: Cut the Money Wasters

When you did the "Budget Planner" worksheet and took inventory of all your expenses, you might have identified one or two memberships that you have set up as a direct debit but you don't use. Did you have any listed on the worksheet? If you use all of the memberships and you are still left with no savings, then identify which are a luxury and can be cut out.

For example, if you pay ninety dollars a month for TV, then see if you can cut it out completely and just use free TV. If you think you are going to miss out on your favorite shows, all the better because you will have that extra time every day to pursue your passions. Or maybe you have multiple channel subscriptions— Netflix, Amazon Prime, cable tv. How about you keep one and cut the most expensive subscriptions? If you think you can't live without TV, then perhaps you can cut the gym membership you don't use every day and instead go for a jog around the park?

A big money waster is food. How much food goes into the trash every week? Reasons range from fresh food that gets spoiled, cooked food that your family and you throw away, cans and preserved food that you thought you might need but have now expired, and so on. The biggest way to cut down on this is to plan your meals and snacks.

How much do women spend on cosmetics that go to waste? From the number of lipsticks to beauty products to nail polish to products in the bathroom. I'm sure there are some things that you can cut down, so they aren't wasted.

How about spending a lot on gadgets? It is so popular to keep regularly updating our phones and laptops and other electronic items, even though they still work. You spend a lot of money without realizing it in trying to "keep up with the Joneses." At one time, I had a laptop for seven years. The only problem was that I had to carry my charger with me, but even when I was finished with it, it was still working perfectly fine. It was a struggle for me to decide if I really wanted a new laptop.

We live in a consumer world—there is always something new coming up and plenty of ads on TV, radio, magazines, and social media to tempt us.

The key is to write a list of your needs vs. wants. To save money, you definitely need to cut out something from the want list, especially if you are constantly living from paycheck to paycheck. This really depends on how much income you make and the size of your family and your important commitments.

Metaphysics is the interesting study of manifestation. The tips in this book are a precursor to help you with manifestation.

Task 4: Automate Savings

As philanthropist investor Warren Buffett said, "Don't save what is left after spending; spend what is left after saving."

Most of you know how much money comes into your bank account every month. So, set up an automatic direct deposit of 10 percent of that into a savings account. Once you do this, then you don't need to worry about putting away money separately as savings.

Susan, a financial planner, highly recommends this strategy. She says, "The power of the compound interest is the eighth wonder of the world.'

Even if it is not 10 percent, start with a set amount each paycheck and increase it as you can.

Bear this in mind: When it comes to savings, it is simple. It really comes to putting away a part of what you earn. It is as simple as that.

If your bank lets you have multiple accounts for minimal fees, then create accounts for your savings, for your luxury spending, for your everyday bills, and so on. That way, you know that your income is automatically split into categories and you don't need to make the effort to do it every time. Dr. Jillian, a successful entrepreneur, advocates this, and it has helped them to keep track of their money.

Task 5: Track Your Spending

Do you find it hard to keep track of your spending? One way to make it easier is to withdraw cash from your checking account that is required for your weekly spending. Spend only that. Bills are usually paid online, so there's no point withdrawing cash for those payments (unless you pay bills physically).

If you withdraw $200 per week for your weekly shopping, and you manage to save $25, then you can either pop it into your savings account (if you are that disciplined) or use that as your allowance for the week.

This is exactly what Helen used to do. After a low point, she slowly rebuilt her life. She worked two jobs and was determined to become financially independent. She withdrew cash from her bank account each week and used it for her weekly spending. At that point in her life, she never went out for coffee or to eat at restaurants. She ate healthy, homecooked meals a lot. These days, now that she is well on her way to managing her money, she knows where she wants to spend her money.

We all live in a world where smartphone have become the norm. There are apps on a smartphone that can track your spending when linked to your bank account. If you set a spending limit, and you only use your debit card to purchase items, the app sends alerts when you have reached or are close to your limit.

The key is to stick with one the methods above, so it helps you monitor your spending and stay on track.

Now that we have covered some tips on creating habits for saving money, why don't you go through the list for your other goals and create tasks for those too?

GOALS

S pecific

M easurable

A chievable

R ealistic

T ime Based

Simple savings that are possible every week.

(For example, put away five dollars per week.)

....

....

....

....

Savings goal to achieve every month.

(For example, cut out one visit to restaurants and put it in your savings jar.)

....

....

....

....

Money wasters that can be cut permanently.

(For example, the pay TV channel that consumes your time or the unused gym membership.)

....

....

....

....

Keep Yourself Inspired

One of the best ways to keep moving forward on this journey to better your life is to constantly put good thoughts and inspiring talks into your brain. Repetitive actions and reminders keep you focused on the task at hand.

Here are some tips to help keep you inspired to achieve your goals.

1. **Share your goals with family and friends.** Once you share your goals with people around you, you are more committed to achieving them because of the pressure on you to succeed. Humans don't like to disappoint people who care about them. But be wary of who you share with, because the last thing you want is someone to demotivate you.

2. **Have someone to hold you accountable.** At work, when we have someone to hold us accountable, we are productive. Similarly, team up with someone who will hold you accountable to reach your goals. You can even do this with a like-minded friend.

3. **Surround yourself with like-minded people.** How many of us stick to the same set of friends just because? Many times, we are comfortable moving around the same set of people we know. Once you start this new pattern of being conscious, you will notice a lot—things and people that don't suit your new thinking.

You don't need to totally stop meeting your friends. If there is one person in your group of friends who is always negative, choose not to interact with this him or her. Or you be the positive one in the group, responding to every negative thing this other person has to say. Over time, three things can happen. This person will change a little, you will stop noticing this person, or you will feel inclined to meet your other friends without this person.

Coffee catch-ups with inspiring people are one of my favorite things to do. Once a month, pick someone you admire and ask them if you can buy coffee and chat with them. This really helps you stay positive and inspired. I have to warn you that this can become addictive. Sometimes, busy people don't have the time to meet you. Make the best use of technology. Suggest a half-hour Skype or Zoom video chat, so it saves time for both of you.

4. **Change is constant, embrace it.** When you write your goals, be aware that sometimes life changes, and it is okay to go with the flow. If you wonder what the point of setting goals is—let me explain it this way. Is your life, right now, what you expected it to be three years ago? How about one year ago? Life happens, relationships happen, and things change.

If, for example, after reading this book, you realize that you actually don't need to be a millionaire to be happy, that is totally okay. The whole point is to actually set one-year goals and work on them consistently. You can then update your goals every year.

Another kind of change is changing the method. If you have tried one way to achieve your goal and it is not working, find another way to make it work. For example, if you tried going to the gym to lift weights and that is not working, try joining a class for Zumba, kickboxing, or yoga. Whatever works for you.

Many of us think that because we committed to exercise and the gym, it has to be just that. If we slip up with this, we say, "Oh, well, I just can't keep up my goals. It's too hard!" Change your thinking and change your habits.

We know that most gyms lock a member into a contract. Rather than sign up for a twelve-month contract, choose a free trial period. If that works, then choose a short-term contract, say three months. Once you know this is for you, then sign up for the twelve-month contract. On the other hand, after the free trial, if you know gym membership is not for you, then choose another style of physical activity. But don't be lazy.

5. **Stop watching the news.** No news is good news these days. TV stations have always aimed to get their ratings up through the delivery of bad news, locally and globally. I am sure there are plenty of good things happening too. The media has created this culture to keep people on the edge and think that the world is a big bad place to live in. As if they can't find any good that is happening! I felt suffocated with all this, a long time ago, even when I was in India, and stopped watching the news—way before I came to Australia. Well, I found that Australian news is no different from Indian news—the pattern hasn't changed.

It is the same with radio, newspapers, magazines, and social media. It seems they too are only after popularity and can't seem to deliver too much inspiring content. Reality TV shows are the worst kind of energy drains, and they do get you addicted. I know it is hard to totally stop watching TV, especially if you are used to it. Try to limit your TV time and instead use it for other tasks, like family time and personal time for growth.

Replace driving or travel time with listening to podcasts or TED talks. There is so much inspiring content available that can help you rewire your brain for positivity.

If you prefer reading, borrow self-development books from the library or use your electronic device to read.

Fiction can be more exciting and romantic, but it does little to help you create a positive life. Again, if you love fiction, limit your books to one a month and allocate more time to reading uplifting content online and/or offline.

For every activity you do, the key thing is to be conscious. Most activities you do, you have developed the habit subconsciously. Develop conscious habits that will propel you in the right direction.

6. **Write a letter to yourself.** Write from the future–from when you have achieved your goals. Write in detail how your life looks one year from now, when you have achieved your goals. Include as much detail as you can. The new habits you have gained, your positive mindset (how you do it), how you spend your day from when you wake up till you go to bed, how you handled your ups and downs, your relationships, your attitude towards life, your spending culture, and the savings in your bank account.

Similar to Jim Carrey's journey, this can be your motivation when you are stuck on your path to greatness or at times of despair.

7. **Increase your savings to pay off your bad debt.** We learned about good debts and bad debts in Part 1 of this book. As you keep saving, try to pay off the high-interest debt. As you slowly achieve this, you will feel a great sense of achievement.

I believe our lives are perfect just the way they are, all of which is created by our thoughts. If we change our thinking and count our gratitude more often, it will bring about more of what we are grateful for.

Here, I recall a short story. There was a boy whose family was wealthy. One day, his father took him on a trip to the countryside. He aimed to show his son how poor people live. They arrived at the farm of a poor family (or someone they thought was poor) and stayed there for a few days. On their return, the father asked his son if he liked the trip.

"Oh, it was great, Dad!" said the son.

"Did you see how the poor people lived?" asked the dad. He asked his son to give his impressions of the trip.

"Well, we only have one dog, while they have four. In our garden, we have a pool, while they have the river with no end. We have expensive lights, but they have stars above their heads in the night sky. We only have a small piece of land, while they have endless fields. We buy food, but they grow it. We have a high fence for protection of our property, but their friends protect it for them."

The father was stunned. He couldn't say a word.

The moral of the story is that sometimes you have everything, but you still feel poor. If you were an optimist, you might say that even though the rich people thought the poor people were poor, they actually were not. They were leading happy, rich lives in their thoughts and in real life, unlike the "rich people" who had poor thoughts.

Happiness is how you feel inside, regardless of what is in your outside world.

Stage 5
Persevere and Review Regularly

"Many of life's failures are people who did not realize how close they were to success when they gave up."

–Thomas A. Edison

When Harland Sanders was five years old, his father died. His mother had to go to work, leaving Sanders to cook and care for his siblings. By the age of seven, he was really good with cooking. When he was ten, he started working as a farmhand. By grade seven, he had dropped out of school and started working at a nearby farm.

For the next twenty years, Sanders shuffled between the life of a farmer, streetcar conductor, soldier, railroad firefighter, lawyer, insurance salesperson, steamboat operator, and a number of other jobs. When he was forty years old, he was running a service station in Kentucky.

Does the name ring a bell? Anyway, let me continue the story. His gas station did not have a restaurant, so he served dinners in his attached personal living quarters. He cooked chicken dishes and other country meals. His dishes were really good, especially his secret chicken recipe. After a while, he opened a restaurant nearby.

As he advertised his food, a fight with his competitor resulted in a shootout. He still did not give up. Four years later, he bought a motel, which burned to the ground along with his restaurant. Yet again, he kept going. He built another motel and restaurant with bigger and better seating capacity.

By the age of fifty, he had perfected his secret recipe for frying chicken in a pressure fryer. The next ten years, he worked at various jobs, one was as a manager at a North Corbin, Kentucky, motel and restaurant, where he started offering his secret recipe.

When he was sixty-two years old, he franchised his secret recipe "Kentucky Fried Chicken" for the first time. His first franchise resulted in the restaurant tripling its profits. Soon other people wanted to offer this fried chicken at their restaurants.

During this time, Sanders believed that his North Corbin restaurant would remain successful indefinitely. But at sixty-five, he had to sell it, because the new interstate reduced customer traffic.

Worried about how his meager $105-a-month pension would help him survive, he set out to find restaurants that would franchise his secret recipe. He wanted a nickel for each piece of chicken sold. The story goes that his recipe was rejected 1,009 times before he finally found his first partner.

The franchise approach became highly successful and Sanders, at seventy-two, obtained a patent to protect his method of pressure frying his chicken. When he was seventy-three, he sold the KFC corporation for two million dollars.

This real-life story beautifully illustrates perseverance and wanting to achieve a goal at any cost. I am not sure if most of us are that tenacious!

It is one thing to learn new habits and set goals, but unless you can keep up the habit, you will end up going back to your previous life–much quicker than you thought was possible. That is why it is important to persevere and do a review regularly on where you are and where you are going. It is so important to not lose that vision you created for yourself, just like Colonel Sanders!

I really hope you took some time to create your goals. Initially, review your goals every week. At the end of the week, check if you have ticked off your task lists for that week. It could have been as simple as putting away money from that one cup of coffee you decided not to buy. This is still progress.

Once you make a change and it becomes a habit, you then don't need to review the goals as often. You can move on to monthly reviews and then to quarterly reviews. Anything less than that might let you slip back into your old ways.

Let's look at how to persevere to keep going with these beautiful new habits we want to gain.

Here are my four powerful ways on how to persevere.

Powerful Strategy 1: Stay Optimistic

Things don't *always* go *exactly* as you plan. You sometimes face unanticipated challenges or things just don't happen as fast or as easily as you'd like them to. This is called life.

You might have had a plan to save fifty dollars this week and an unexpected sickness in the family made you spend some money on antibiotics. You might be slightly disappointed with this. Or perhaps last week you had to use your credit card to replace your washing machine from eight years ago.

That is totally okay.

The most important thing we need in our life is to stay as optimistic as possible, even when things don't go as planned. Because the more you live life, the more you'll see that things usually happen *differently* than you expected. But they do happen for the best and usually they turn out quite well. Take on the mentality that this is the way the universe will test your commitment to your goal. This can happen when just starting out to when you are at the pinnacle of success. Stay rationally optimistic.

Have a friend you can call when you feel down. Surround yourself with people who can uplift you when needed.

Powerful Strategy 2: Embrace Setbacks

We are all human beings, and we all have our good days and our bad days. This is a combination of our body (as in health), our mind, and the environment (relationships, politics, work, and family).

Most millionaires, billionaires, and hugely successful people say that some of their greatest setbacks were important lessons to their success.

But how do you actually embrace setbacks without feeling a let-down?

My top tip is to just let yourself experience the feeling that accompanies the setback. Be it tears of sadness or anger, just let them flow. Sometimes, we don't even know why we are crying (is that true, women?), but you know it makes you feel better afterwards. So be it. If you have a shoulder to cry on, that's even better.

If anger is your emotion, have a punching bag at hand to punch out your anger or take a stick and beat at the ground till you feel the emotion subside. (Crying is my favorite way to release my emotions, but you can release your emotions however you want.)

Sometimes, setbacks can be hard, like the loss of a loved one. In this case, it might take ages to get over it. Think about a husband and wife who have been together for fifty years. That is a long time together, and the spouse needs to get over it. There are good days and really bad days, but the idea is to surround yourself with friends and people who can support you.

Just by letting our body experience the emotion, we are first and foremost accepting that there is a setback and it is okay for us to go through it. What we are also telling ourselves is that this is a temporary thing, and it too shall pass.

Lack of money in an emergency can be one of the biggest setbacks that can make you feel frustrated. That is exactly what you are working on in your life, through this book. I am so glad that you want to make that change, so do keep going. But when you are stuck for lack of money, and you are doing everything you can, know that the universe has your back and will do everything to help you.

When it does, you know deep down that you will figure out whatever it is, and life will be much better.

So, don't suppress your emotions. If you have a setback, embrace it and learn from it. The "can do" attitude that follows is the most important thing to embrace setbacks.

One piece of advice here: Don't be stuck with the negative emotion for too long. This can take you into a downward spiral. How long is too long? There is no one answer. It depends on the event.

Powerful Strategy 3: Take Breaks

One other powerful strategy to help you get through setbacks is meditation and journaling.

We covered destressing in a previous section. Don't drive yourself to the ground by stressing all the time to achieve your goals.

Life, in general, is fast paced in today's world. There is so much to do every single day. Work is top priority. Combining it with achieving goals can just be the last straw for you.

It is important to take a break. This can range from going for a walk to taking a holiday. Sometimes, we get so caught up trying to achieve a goal that we forget to enjoy the process. We get stressed about what we are not able to achieve. Or we fail to acknowledge minute progress.

Often, our greatest insights and creative solutions come during those moments when we give ourselves a break. We now know that Einstein achieved many of his groundbreaking creative insights during his "downtime," when he wasn't hard at work in the lab.

Your brain works the same way as Einstein's did (we humans are all fundamentally built the same way). So, next time you're in need of a truly creative solution or a "groundbreaking idea" for your goal, do the counterintuitive thing—take a relaxing break.

Powerful Strategy 4: Realize You Are Exactly Where You Need to Be

One thing I have learned over time is to believe in this wisdom—"Realize you are exactly where you need to be." Sometimes, you might try so hard to achieve a goal, and it doesn't go as planned. At other times, you don't even try that hard and everything seems to flow quite smoothly. You achieve the same thing with ease.

The universe or God or whatever higher power/energy you believe in gives you exactly what you need at the right time. This is a part of the trusting process we all need to undertake.

Besides, when you are close to achieving your goal, oftentimes you are ready to set your next goal. Are you not? Such is life. So, don't beat yourself up about not getting there fast enough!

Just enjoy your journey and the process. Understand where you stand now is meant to be exactly that way on your path of success.

Regular Review Is Key to Success

The last step to successfully take control of your money management is to periodically evaluate and revise your plan.

When you initially start saving, check once a week to see if you have achieved your savings goal. Compare your planned spending and saving with your actual spending and saving for the week. This step will help you measure your progress towards your goals.

If you find that you are not reaching your goals, you will need to answer these questions.

- Are my goals still important?
- Is my financial goal too ambitious?

If the goals are still important to you, then ask yourself if the goal is too ambitious. Consider these questions.

- Is the planned savings amount reasonable?
- Was spending out of control in one or more areas?

If so, change tactics to control spending in that area. For example, if you had eaten out more often, understand why that was the case. Was it because you failed to preplan your meals, did you get lazy, was it a night when someone was sick?

Understand and Adjust Your Goals as Needed

As you get better with your savings, you might only need to review the goal once a month, and then gradually review it quarterly.

How else can you save/earn more?

It is important to spend less than what you earn. Initially, that is how you can get seed capital to invest in property or shares or any kind of investment. It can also help you with creating an emergency fund.

If you already have some control over your money and want to make it grow, then why not? This is where investments can help. From stocks to shares to property, there are various ways to grow your wealth.

Most people don't invest at all because it is too scary to choose the vehicle of investment. But what if there is an expert in that field who can guide you to grow your money? They are called financial planners.

Some financial planners have a bad reputation for misleading people. But find an honest person who can help you, and that is one of the best ways to grow your money and help you plan for retirement.

Maybe you are in a job now where you earn money and you know you have the potential to earn more. Have you ever asked for a pay raise at work, or are you assuming that you are not going to get paid more? "Ask and you shall receive."

The worst-case scenario is you have asked for what you think you are worth. Two things can come out of this. One, you will realize your true value. Two, you will look for a job where you will be compensated for what you are worth.

The key is be well-connected. Attend networking events to find a potential recruiter to land that dream job you want. Build connections—it is always about who you know, rather than what you know.

In today's technologically connected world, it has become easier to find ways to make money. You can make money online by offering your services part-time. Spending an hour online doing tasks you are good at, from the comfort of your home, can help you earn hundreds or thousands of dollars a week. Who knows? This might give you the freedom and lifestyle you want to live and one day you might be in a position to quit your job that requires being at a certain place every day.

You can also use your hobby to bring in extra income. Do you love baking cakes? Start off with small projects by baking cakes for people you know and charging them for it. Being really good at what you do will make others want your services.

Dispose of extra things you actually don't need to bring in some extra cash. Do this every year to bring in some cash for the holiday season.

50 Easy Ways to Save Money

Touchy-Feely Stuff

1. Have a written budget—this is the easiest way to know where your money goes and where you can cut down to save.
2. Get your partner (if you have one) onboard. When two people are like-minded, it is much easier to keep on track.
3. Learn how to cope with stress without spending. Every time you feel like shopping or smoking due to stress, try taking a walk or go for a run instead.
4. Learn to say "no" and don't feel pressured to do what everyone else is doing. If your kids want to eat out too much or friends want you to go to the movies every week, it is up to you to decide if you want to or not.

Food

5. Write a weekly meal menu and cut down on waste. Doing this means a once-a-week shopping trip and also less food waste.
6. Make your own lunches by cooking double portions and freezing the other half. Soups, lasagna, bolognaise sauce, and curries all freeze well.
7. Use a shopping list app to help you keep on track. Apps are available on smartphones or create a simple shopping list as

a note on your smartphone helps keep a running shopping list.

8. Buy your own coffee machine to save money and make coffee your way.

9. Take your own lunch to work. This one tip can save you up to $1,000 per year! (ten dollars for lunch, times five working days, times fifty weeks a year equals $2,500 savings a year).

10. Similarly, packing school lunches can save hundreds of dollars a year.

11. Bottle your own water by having a drink bottle and refilling from the tap or a cooler.

12. Frozen veggies are a good way to save money and waste. Frozen veggies are not inferior to fresh; frozen peas, corn, and beans are good and easy to use.

13. Go grocery shopping on a full stomach, because your brain will tend to stick to the list you made rather than impulse buying.

Banks, Insurance, and Pensions

14. Pay your bills on time and save up to ten dollars per late payment per bill.

15. Monitor your bank balance for any unusual activity and to make sure you haven't been charged late fees.

16. Check how much interest rate you are paying on your credit card. It ranges from 10 percent to 22 percent, so changing to a low-interest rate card can save hundreds of dollars a year.

17. Contact your bank and ask for a lower interest rate or use a good mortgage broker to get a good rate on an ongoing basis.

18. Shop around for car, health, and personal insurance to save hundreds or thousands of dollars a year.

19. Review your pension; even a small difference in fees helps you save money.

Around the Home

20. Review and update your telephone plans. There are so many plans that are inexpensive and provide cost-effective benefits.
21. Install energy-efficient light bulbs. Changing bulbs to LED globes can save money.
22. Choose energy-efficient appliances; it might cost slightly higher upfront but will save a lot in energy bills over time.
23. Be vigilant around electronics. If you are bored, refrain from turning on the TV—instead, read a book or go for a walk!
24. Clean the top, sides, and back of your fridge. Blocked vents make the fridge less efficient and increase energy bills.

Transportation

25. Washing your own car can save forty-five dollars or more every time.
26. Use top-quality fuel, if your vehicle allows it. Even though it is expensive upfront, it is more energy efficient in the long run.
27. Use public transportation to save money and reduce your carbon footprint.
28. Check your car tires regularly. This can result in saving money on fuel.
29. Carpool when you can—either to work or nights with friends.

Being Organized

30. Organize your receipts so you can claim tax deductions.
31. Join an online budgeting community to help you keep motivated.

32. Track lost money in bank accounts, shares, or life insurance policies.
33. Check your calendar to preplan gift purchases so you don't overspend on last-minute purchases.
34. Cancel memberships you don't use.
35. Delete online credit card numbers, so you don't automatically buy things.
36. Try working with cash only. No credit or debit cards. Withdraw cash each week and make it last as long as you can. Anything leftover goes into savings!

Behavior Changes

37. When shopping at stores, use layaway, by paying a deposit to hold the item, instead of buying the item on credit. This helps you change your mind on those impulsive, expensive shopping trips.
38. Start a coin jar. Who doesn't like to see money being saved? Throw your coins into a jar at the end of each day. If you don't carry cash, open a high-interest earning savings account.
39. Use your local library to borrow items, instead of purchasing books, e-books, CDs, and DVDs.
40. If all else fails and you love impulse buying, calculate how many hours you have to work to be able to purchase what you are after! Maybe you will think twice.
41. Don't be quick to trash things. If your jeans rip, turn them into the latest fashion or try to mend them (if you are like me and don't like ripped jeans).
42. Go to free events with your children to make it fun for everyone. Go to the park or play in your backyard rather than pay money for entertainment.
43. Clothes can be less expensive if you purchase them online

or wait for sales.

44. Purchase the generic version of medicines and don't pay extra for the brand name.

45. Sign up for free customer rewards and receive cashback benefits, discounts, and other rewards.

46. Try to have parties at your home and save considerably on food and drinks (especially alcohol).

47. Don't ignore the spare change in your purse and use that to purchase coffee.

48. Designate yourself as the driver when you head out. You will save money and keep your friends safe.

49. Do your own yard work or gardening instead of paying someone else. It's great exercise for you and helps you connect with nature.

50. Do the stuff on this list. I'm serious, just reading these tips is one thing, but action is the real thing. So, try a few for yourself.

50 Ways to Earn More Money

1. Get paid to be a mystery shopper.

2. Create YouTube videos using your knowledge or talent to attract a lot of visitors.

3. Earn extra money doing part-time what you like doing now outside your normal job.

4. Sell used clothes that you don't wear.

5. Drive passengers with Uber, Lyft, or other car services.

6. Sell extra CDs, DVDs, video games, and electronics.

7. Sell unwanted jewelry.

8. Use loyalty programs to earn points and purchase items.

9. Do virtual jobs online from the comfort of your home.
10. Check for coins with specific designs or with strange serial numbers; you might come across an antique that people are ready to pay lots of money for.
11. Share your expertise by launching an online resource.
12. Work part-time for customer-service jobs from home!
13. If you are good with English, do part-time writing or editing to earn money.
14. Write an article for websites that pay you.
15. Are you a good listener and typist? Work as a transcriptionist.
16. If you are good with grammar, proofread documents and get paid for your work.
17. If you have a smartphone and love photography, sell your pictures to earn cash.
18. Rent your clothing.
19. If you love to play chess (or any game), tutor online to make money.
20. If you love cooking, start a blog. Eventually, ads will bring in extra cash.
21. Leverage the power of Amazon (sell products that you might not even see).
22. Leverage your spare bedroom by renting it out through Airbnb. You can end up earning a few thousand dollars based on where you live.
23. Coordinate events—like Meetup—and share knowledge. If done right, without a speaker, you can make some money by selling tickets.
24. Tutor high school or university students and monetize your expertise.
25. Make money using your artsy talent.
26. If you love to cook, you can sell healthy, home-cooked meals to earn money.
27. Wash cars—even if you don't own one.

28. Walk dogs for your neighbors and other busy people for a fee.
29. Mow lawns or help with gardening. Many people don't have the time to plant a veggie patch; if you know how to, help them.
30. Sell an online course—use your knowledge to create a course and sell it on learning websites, like Udemy.
31. Switch banks to save money, especially if you are paying a lot in fees.
32. Shop around for cheaper utilities (electric, gas, water, trash, phones, pay TV). Do this at least once every two years.
33. Sell your used books.
34. If you are musically gifted, you can play or sing with a band.
35. You can do public speaking to earn extra cash!
36. If you love sales, maybe you can do a part-time sales jobs over the weekend.
37. If you are a fitness freak, monetize it by offering weekend fitness classes.
38. If you love babies, you can offer childcare and earn money.
39. If organizing comes naturally to you, offer it as a paid service. So many people just don't have the time to keep their place organized and tidy.
40. If you are good at building websites, do it as a side project. Maybe one day you will make more from this than your day job!
41. If you love writing, you can author books (adult, fiction, nonfiction, or children's stories) and sell them online as an independent author.
42. Resell thrift store items.
43. Do odd jobs that you offer online through social media sites.
44. Take free items from online sites or that are placed at the roadside. Sell them to make money
45. Take surveys and watch ads that offer you money.
46. Use the Amazon Mechanical Turk crowdsourcing website. Do odd jobs to make some extra cash

47. You can deliver pizzas in your spare time and get paid.
48. You can use your vehicle and get paid to make deliveries.
49. Draw caricatures at events or weekend markets.
50. Be an extra on TV shows and get paid.

A word of caution. Be sure to check your local, state, and federal rules to follow the laws for any of these activities. Some governments have strict guidelines about selling food, working with children, and receiving money for certain activities.

Charity

One last thing I want to include in this section is about charity and giving.

Often, the basic things we take for granted–like food, clothing, and shelter–are the things that millions of people don't have. When we take time to think about others in need, it highlights what we have in our lives. This, in turn, makes us count our blessings and feel grateful.

Giving regularly will bring more of what you want in your life.

If you aim to save five dollars a week–as a bare minimum–give away one dollar of it to the needy. See what joy it brings to someone and how it lights up their face when you give what you can, be it $50 or $500.

Choose to give to a registered charity, through a religious organization, or a government-sponsored institution.

One other thing you can do to feel grateful is to volunteer–give your time.

Of all the resources we have, time is the only resource that cannot be bought. It is so precious. Choose to give some of it by doing volunteer work, wherever your heart is or whichever cause you feel close to. Again, the joy this brings to both the receiver and the giver is immeasurable.

Let me share an illustration of this concept. One day after a high tide, a lot of starfish washed up on the shore. They started drying up and dying. A little boy who happened to pass that way started throwing the starfish, one at a time, back into the sea, so that they could live a little longer.

A man came up to him and asked, "What are you doing? Look around. Your efforts won't make a difference, there are thousands of dying starfish."

The boy, without breaking stride, picked up another starfish. Before throwing it back, he replied, "Well, it will make a difference to this one" and continued with his efforts.

Do not underestimate the power of your deeds.

PART 3

FURTHER CONSIDERATIONS

Money and Happiness

We have been conditioned to believe that the richer we are, the happier we will be. But, is there actually a correlation between money and happiness? Many studies have shown that after the $75,000 per annum mark, there is not much difference in the level of happiness.

And then you hear things like, "I'd rather be rich and crying on my private boat, than be poor and crying on the streets." These kinds of statements have led us to believe that it is better to be rich and sad than be poor and happy.

What if both are not true?

What if the secret lies in finding out exactly what your version of rich means, so that you can work towards it? Because with that understanding comes power—power to realize that your version of being rich might not be that daunting. It is not an exhausting number you have in your head right now.

Ready to take the challenge with me?

Setting Goals to Save

My belief is that you always need to spend less than you earn, so you can use the extra money to grow your wealth and have some fun too—*live life*.

Before I move on to the specifics about how you can do this for yourself, let me tell you a little bit about financial literacy.

Financial literacy encompasses knowing about money matters and being equipped to utilize that knowledge by applying it across a range of contexts. What a person needs to know to be financially literate will vary depending on his or her circumstances and needs.

Generally, however, it will involve an understanding of the following details.

- A person's values and priorities.
- Budgeting, savings, and how to manage money.
- Credit.
- Insurance and protecting against risk.
- Investment basics.
- Pensions.
- Retirement planning.
- Benefits of shopping around and how to compare products.
- Where to go for advice and additional information, guidance, and support.
- How to recognize a potential conflict of interest.
- How to recognize and avoid scams.

In this book, my aim is to provide you ways and means to improve your mindset and lifestyle to consistently achieve your savings goals. I am not a financial planner and do not intend to advise you how to grow your wealth. However, I do realize the importance of some of the other financial skills that you need to acquire to grow your wealth or at least use the services of professionals.

Let's assume you have a trip planned in the next twelve months and you need to save $5,000 for the trip. Let's also assume that you are single and have an income of $80,000 or more. (Don't worry, if your income is less. Everyone is different and your spending can always be adjusted based on your income).

If you are single and conscious about your spending, this should be a relatively easy task. If you are anything like me, when someone says, "You can't do it," you always make sure you achieve the goal, but you also go over and above. But, if you have struggled in the past, then you need to start somewhere. So, let this book be your motivation to start small. The average rule is that you save 10 percent of whatever you earn.

Whatever number your goal is, you then break it down further to see how much you need to save every month. So, looking at this monthly, it comes to about $416 a month. You can further break it down to weekly and aim to save $104 a week.

Think about weekday lunches (ten dollars times five days equals fifty dollars), weekday coffees (four dollars times five days equals twenty dollars), weekend eating out (thirty dollars), Friday night drinks with friends (twenty to thirty dollars). There's $120–$130 per week that you can possibly save. For those of you who say, "I don't buy my lunch every day, I bring homecooked food," think about other areas where you are spending. Is it over the weekend at the pub with friends, or do you tend to eat out most nights, or do you spend too much on cosmetics, clothes, or shoes?

If you don't know your priorities, in the simplest terms, how will you know where to spend and where to save? I have never suggested that people live like scrooges. Rather, it is being wise with your money or more like practicing the concept of "allocating money into different baskets" and have some leftover for you to spend. That too is on *your* priorities, not what somebody else expects you to do (as in social pressure).

Okay, so how do you budget and understand your monthly living expenses?

If this is your first time creating a budget, I suggest looking at your bills over the last six months or even over the last year. If you have internet banking, this can be a little easier than with manual bills. Use a budget calculator spreadsheet to make note of your fixed expenses every month (rent or mortgage, vehicle loans, personal loans, insurance, gym subscriptions, others). For varying expenses—like utilities, groceries, eating out, clothes and shoes—look at a one-year history—see how much you spent every month and then take an average.

Some bills are paid annually—which is why it is good to go back and check your expenses over a year rather than a short term.

Don't forget that cup of coffee you buy using cash! Think about what else you use cash for. Parking? Ice cream for children (or yourself).

Typically, write what you do day in and day out—for a whole week. Look at Monday to Friday—the working week and then the weekend.

Once you have taken some time to do this, you can check this with the numbers that you entered on the prework "Budget Planner" worksheet and compare to see if you knew exactly where your money was being spent.

If there is a big variance, it means you are not aware of your expenditures. The first step is to acknowledge that something needs to change for you to take control of your money.

Now, go over your budget and see where you can cut expenses. If you are addicted to shoes and clothes and buy them once a week or once a month, that is not a need, it is a want! If spending on wants is predominantly using credit cards, then you really need to cut your credit card spending and learn to only live within your means.

Similarly, if you buy lunch outside and your excuse is that you are busy over the weekend and have no time to prep, ask yourself what you are busy with over the weekend. Do you really work seven days a week, or do you not have enough help with other chores that you are too tired for meal prep?

Remember the limiting beliefs that you wrote down in the "Step 1 Worksheet What are your limiting beliefs?" Link your ability to save (or not save) to these beliefs. It will help clarify why you have to cut down on spending.

Once you do this, you will find ways to reduce your spending and increase your savings.

Congratulations! You have taken the first step to take control of your money!

But it doesn't stop here. Remember "action is critical." So, please take time to understand where your money is being spent over the budgeted limit and then create an ideal budget for yourself.

Okay, before you think this is all too hard, I want to show you how you don't have to earn millions of dollars to live your dream life.

Before we start, write down on a piece of paper the amount of money in your bank that will help you live your absolute dream life. Go on, be bold, and write how much money will let you live carefree.

Now, use the "How Much Money Do You Actually Need to Live Your Dream Life? Worksheet" and fill in the numbers there. To know exactly what you need, you should have first completed the "Budget Planner" worksheet. Otherwise, it will only be assumptions and not concrete numbers.

For example, I live in Australia. According to the Australian Securities & Investments Commission (ASIC) MoneySmart website (2016), a person who is single and under thirty-five years of age, will spend an average of $849 per month. The extra luxuries and holiday/charity spending will vary for each person.

So, I've made assumptions here. Let's break it down.

Basic Necessities

Rent or mortgage payment	$1,230.00 per month
Food/groceries	$600.00 per month
Utilities (gas, electric, water, phone, TV)	$104.00 per month
Medical and health	$100.00 per month
Transportation	$420.00 per month
Insurance payments	$40.00 per month
Total	$2,494.00 per month
Total basic monthly expense:	$2,494.00 x 12 = $29,928.00 per year (A)

Money for Extra Luxuries

Clothing and footwear	$78.00 per month
Recreation	$359.67 per month
Alcohol	$95.33 per month
Total	$533.00 per month
Total basic monthly expense:	$533.00 x 12 = $6,396.00 per year (B)

Holidays and Charity

Monthly donation to charity	$35.00 per month
Holidays	$200.00 per month
Total	$235.00 per month
Total basic monthly expense:	$235.00 x 12 = $2,820.00 per year (C)

Add (A), (B), and (C) together equals $39,144 per year.

These numbers are an average and an assumption amount of what a single person needs to live. Complete the worksheet below using your expenses to find out what your numbers are.

How Much Money Do You Actually Need to Live Your Dream Life? Worksheet

Basic Necessities

Rent or mortgage payment	$_____ per month
Food/groceries	$_____ per month
Utilities (gas, electric, water, phone, TV)	$_____ per month
Medical and health	$_____ per month
Transportation	$_____ per month
Insurance payments	$_____ per month
Total	$_____ per month

Total basic monthly expense:

$_____ x 12 = $_____ **per year (A)**

Money for Extra Luxuries

Clothing and footwear	$_____ per month
Recreation	$_____ per month
Alcohol	$_____ per month
Total	$_____ per month

Total basic monthly expense:

$_____ x 12 = $_____ **per year (B)**

Holidays and Charity

Monthly donation to charity	$_____ per month
Holidays	$_____ per month
Total	$_____ per month

Total basic monthly expense:

$_____ x 12 = $_____ **per year (C)**

Add (A), (B), and (C) together equals $_____ per year.

Divide this by twelve and you will get the monthly income you need to live on. If you use these figures to extrapolate, you will know how much money you need as passive income when you retire (bearing in mind your situation might be quite different then).

What Do You Do with the Money You Save?

Really, it's not that hard to spend money, I hear you say.

Here are my top eight reasons.

1. Pay Off/Manage Debts

Quite often, when you hear about trying to save money and you are already struggling with managing day-to-day cash flow, it can be overwhelming. You might have credit card debts and maybe a car loan and a personal loan. This can be an extreme situation. But most of you probably have at least one credit card debt and a car loan. In certain situations, even without a home mortgage loan, you might be struggling to pay off the credit card debts every month, only paying the minimum due. This is a dangerous way to live!

If this is something that represents your life at this time, then saving money is even more important to slowly reduce your debts. Do you like the stress of opening bills every month and not having enough to pay off your debts?

No one likes living from paycheck to paycheck.

This one reason should be enough to prompt you to start saving and aim to have less or no more bad debt.

2. Fun Money

Who doesn't like to have fun? I certainly do! We all need money for those occasional coffee catch-ups with our friends. How about some indulgence and pampering yourself with or without your girlfriends?

3. Travel

Most people love traveling. How often do you travel—maybe once a year? After you came back from your holiday and your credit card bill arrived, did you panic and think that you might have to live on beans for the next month or two? How good does it sound that you could go on a trip and when you come back, you don't have to worry about the credit card bill because you saved money and paid for everything before you went on this trip. You definitely need to save up before you travel.

4. Emergency Funds

This is a big expense that many people fail to understand the impact of. An emergency can be health, household, or vehicles. Imagine this—it is peak winter and you are living in a cold city. Your hot water system has been acting up recently and you know at some point you need to replace it. One cold, Saturday morning, as you turn on your kitchen tap, the water is not hot anymore. You dread it! Not only does this happen on a weekend, it's also at the time when your credit card is maxed and you don't have any savings!

Do you think this scenario is exaggerated or one that can happen? It is likely that it can happen in any one of your houses.

Or have you ever been stuck because you didn't have enough money to fix your car? How about a health issue and you didn't have insurance?

Whatever your emergency might be, having some savings for an emergency can give you peace of mind.

5. Charity

Many of us like to help the less fortunate. Even though we sometimes go through difficult times, it is definitely in our nature to help someone who is experiencing something worse than we are. It is always better to contribute to charity from our savings.

6. Invest/Grow Wealth

If you want to grow your wealth–be it through property, shares, or any kind of investment, it requires an initial investment. Some of you might be lucky to have parents who are able to help you with deposit/down payment money for a house or have been investing on your behalf from your childhood and the money has grown significantly over the years. But a large percentage of the population is not at that level. So, you definitely need to save money for you to grow your wealth.

7. Children's Education

If you have children or are planning to start a family in the future, you know that raising children definitely involves money–sometimes less, usually more. When it comes to education, the cost is high, especially if you choose private schooling for your children. Unless you plan and save for their education, you can find yourself struggling when the time comes to pay for the schooling.

8. Maternity Leave

Oooh, another big one. If you have been through this journey, you probably relate to the minimal freedom you had (money-wise) between having your baby and returning to work. However much you plan, women are sometimes left behind, and situations can get tough if you don't plan for your maternity leave. There will always be unexpected expenses. Even a coffee with some of the other mothers can be hard when living on one income, if you have not saved up money for this time period. Be wise!

Summary

Money is necessary for essentials and luxuries. It is the predominant method of transaction on this planet with other methods coming about–think bitcoin and cryptocurrency. When our basic necessities have been met and more money comes our way, we want to spend it on luxuries. There is nothing wrong with that.

The problem arises when you think that you will be happy only when you have a lot of money in your bank account. This causes unnecessary stress and tension on your current lifestyle. Instead of living in the present, you start chasing the future and declare that you will not be happy until that time.

Rather than going in circles, how about if you decide to be happy with what you currently have in your life and appreciate everything you have? Every time you pay a bill, instead of complaining, how about if you are thankful for the money in your account to pay that bill? For example, if you pay a bill for utilities, how about you feel gratitude for the heating/cooling or the water that flows when you open the tap? Every time your paycheck goes into your account and you look at it, feel grateful.

What this does is amazing. When you habitually feel gratitude, it brings more of what you are grateful for. When you start doing this for everything that you spend money on, and feel grateful all the time, it creates an amazing wave of gratefulness and brings other benefits to you–better health, more money.

So, take some time to understand your dream list and combine it with gratefulness to see how your life improves for the better.

Couples and Money

However much we might argue that happiness is not linked to money, this is one of the number one stress factors in a relationship.

Many women are choosing to be single for a longer time before they enter into a relationship. The longer you are single, the harder it is to adjust being with another individual. This might not be true for all, but it really depends on your nature. If you are a strong-minded person compared to your partner, then you might find it hard to give in and vice versa.

Here are five common questions that are on women's mind when it comes to relationships and money. This is entirely my opinion and there is no right or wrong way to view this topic. You might or might not agree with me. Feel free to take what suits you.

1. What are the money conversations that women should have with their partners?

In a relationship, there are two people, which means there are two different kinds of personalities, especially when it comes to money. When you are first in love, money is not a topic of importance. But the same "money" can cause so much stress in relationships at a later stage.

Whether you are married or not, maybe you live with a partner, try to be open about your money choices. One of you might be a spendthrift, while the other might be a saver. These are extreme ends and will require a lot of work to find balance. When both of you are shopaholics, that is a disaster when it comes to managing your money. The best kind of relationship would be when both people are savers, but that can be rare. You see how there can be different combinations.

That is why it is best to talk about money openly with your partner, just like you would discuss other things.

Leonara and her husband decided to start their own business. What they didn't take into account was the effect it would have on their personal lives. Only when they hit a low point did they decide to make changes as a family. In a similar situation, Bianca has now taken charge of the family financial affairs and has open and honest conversations with her husband. There is complete transparency and their weekly conversations have helped her get through months that were low, income-wise.

Talk about each of your dreams when it comes to money. Discuss each person's current income, what it would look like in five years, whether you like spending money (eating out/buying things) or you'd prefer to save; what financial freedom means to each of you; how long you would like to work before you retire. The important thing is that this needs to be done without judgment. Because when two different personalities talk, it can be hard for each to understand the "money language" of the other person. The conversation doesn't end there though.

The next step of the discussion needs to be as a family unit. If you are a couple and want to have children, how do you want your financial situation to look at that time? What about schooling, extra-curricular activities? What about taking turns to look after children, so that if the wife wants to grow her career, she too gets an equal opportunity? Will you cut down on expenses with only one income? Is one income enough to meet all your liabilities, or do you need to plan accordingly before having a baby? So many questions, the answers need to be arrived at as a couple–a win-win for both!

2. How can women ensure they have financial independence in relationships?

Financial independence means that I have some money in my account to spend as I wish, without having to be accountable to my partner. In the general sense, I think that is what most women want and men too.

I love the concept of your money–my money–our money. In my opinion, it is good to have one joint account and then each person has his or her own separate account. The first thing is to work out what the family spending looks like (budget). Once this is done, split the figure in half–husband and wife each contribute. As long as there is a surplus, each person gets to keep the leftover money to do what he or she likes.

It can be a little more complicated when incomes are not similar or when the wife is a homemaker. This is where working together as a team with shared goals will help.

Regardless of any situation and how much a woman earns, my suggestion is to put away some money in an emergency fund (separate account) and keep growing the balance for a rainy day–either for yourself or for your family.

3. Are prenups important or when are they not?

There is no right or wrong way. Where I come from (India), prenups are not common. Times have changed, and some people are beginning to take this step before marriage. It can be a cultural thing too. With intercultural marriages becoming more common, if someone asks you to sign a prenup, would you?

There is obviously some benefit to signing a prenup, especially in the Western world where it can be enforced a little bit better than some areas of the world. If you bring a lot to the marriage and want some protection, then prenup is a risk-management strategy. Just like insurance, if it gives you peace of mind, then you should definitely get a prenup.

4. How important are money conversations before kids?

It is important to have a conversation about kids, way before you actually think it is due. As nature would have it, women go through changes in their bodies, and after becoming mothers, their bank balances suffer along with their pensions. Many women do not think that this makes a big difference, but women who decide to have children often have less money than their partners who decide to keep working.

Women need to take into account that during pregnancy there could be times when they might have to finish employment earlier than planned, and, if so, their income will be affected. If you are someone who has been independent (with regard to money) until this time, be aware that unless you have some savings or another plan in place, you will be on one income and there might not be enough money for luxuries that you considered as part of your lifestyle before.

This is exactly what happened to Sadhana when she had her first child. It was hard for her partner and her to change their pre-baby lifestyle. Living on one income, they often ran out of money by the end of the month.

This is why I say these conversations are due way before you plan a baby. Just like you plan and save money when you want to buy a house, it might be wise to plan and save before you have a baby—for costs associated with baby things—and also a separate fund for women to have as pocket money should they wish to continue their weekly coffee catch-ups with friends and so on. This way, they are not dependent on their partner when the time arrives. If you have a really supportive partner, maybe you can take turns with looking after your baby in the first year—just like the New Zealand prime minister, Jacinta Arden, and her partner, Clarke Gayford, did.

5. What are the kinds of discussions women should have with their partners?

Technically, all sorts of discussions—isn't that what a relationship is all about? But in all likelihood and through years of wisdom, I would say that some discussions are for girlfriends and some are to be had with your partner. Not because you don't trust your partner, but because men are from Mars and women are from Venus! This might sound like a cliché, but you know what? We have to agree that we are different—if you whine about something to your husband, you might never receive sympathy or an answer that *you* want to hear. Try the same with your girlfriend and the results will be to your satisfaction.

Jokes apart, if both partners have a good understanding and respect for each other, you should be able to tell your partner anything you want without any apprehension. That doesn't mean that your partner will agree with you every time, but you should still have the confidence to be bold and express your views. As I tell my children, express your views, and learn to say "no" to a family member or anyone—as long as what you are doing feels right to you and doesn't harm anyone. Over time, your partner will come to respect you for your decisions.

This was hard for Christa with her first partner. She grew up with a background of saving to buy anything she wanted, had earned an income since she was thirteen and self-support-ed herself through university. Even though she tried her best, ultimately it was hard for her partner to understand her views and she made the hard decision to leave. Her advice to women is to keep your accounts separate, unless both of you have got the same values, especially in the early years of your relationship.

Ask anyone who has been married for a long time, and they will guarantee that relationships are a lot of give and take. But if you want to make your relationship a happy one, then it is important to have an open mind and be able to converse with your partner about your likes and dislikes. Give and take respect of each other's wishes and preferences in life.

How to Put It All Together

So far, I've discussed a lot of concepts, things to consider—small and large. Sometimes, with all the things you have to do in life, even one more small thing can make you feel that you want to pull out your hair.

Therefore, this summarizing of the book might be helpful to you.

Week 1: Take Stock of Your Current Life

Take a notebook and set aside some time to do this work. It might take you a few sessions to complete the work, but this is essential work to know where you are and to plot a new life, one to your liking.

Worksheet exercises to complete include the "Discovery Exercise," the "Spending Exercise," the "Current Income and Expenses Worksheet," and the "Net Worth Worksheet."

Know that trying to do all these exercises at one time can be overwhelming. If you need to take time, then my suggestion is to complete one exercise per day. This will help you split your time and also have a fresh mind each time to do these exercises. Be aware that the income and expense worksheet can take some time, especially if you are doing it for the first time, so be patient with yourself.

Weeks 2 and 3: Use the I.D.E.A.L. Method to Shift Your Mindset

1. Identify your current limiting beliefs.
2. Discover new empowering beliefs.
3. Engage your response-ability.
4. Adopt a growth mindset.
5. Listen to your inner voice.

Now that you have taken some time to understand your current life, you need to dig a little deeper to find out what is stopping you from achieving your deep desires. Steps one and two of the I.D.E.A.L. method are important to change your current reality and instill new beliefs.

Worksheet exercises to complete include "Step 1 Worksheet, What are your limiting beliefs?"

and the "Step 2 Worksheet, Expose your own limiting beliefs and replace with positive affirmations." I have designed these exercises to be simple enough to do them yourself. The idea is to be honest with yourself. True change requires courage to look within yourself and see what is working and what is not.

Be brave, acknowledge what is not working for you, and dig deep to find the truth.

Sometimes, thoughts come to you during the day when you are doing other things. So, always have your notebook handy to jot down your thoughts.

Once you discover your limiting beliefs, make sure you find alternate empowering beliefs and repeat them over and over until they become the essence of you.

Try repeating this for the next two weeks before you move on to the next steps.

Week 4: Use Steps Three, Four and Five throughout Your Life, Not Just as One-Offs

All these concepts are to become your new way of life. During week four, adopt steps three, four, and five of the I.D.E.A.L. method. Incorporate growth mindset and consciousness in the little things you do in your everyday life.

Weeks 5 and 6: Create New Habits to Support Your Lifestyle

This week, in your notebook, the rubber hits the road. You are looking at your current habits—your morning, night, and weekend routines. You are going to take some time to craft these routines to create habits that will support you on your new journey.

Worksheet exercises to complete include "Your Current Lifestyle Worksheet" and "Create Your New Lifestyle Worksheet."

You are then going to create some non-negotiables in your life. For the next two weeks, I urge you to follow these rituals in your life and see the difference they make.

Week 7: Set Goals That You Want

This week, you are going to look at what is important in your life to you, at this stage (not five years ago or not what someone else wants for you). You are going to look at eight categories (money and finance, business/career, relationships, health and wellness, recreation and play, personal and spiritual, personal environment, service and contribution) and set goals for each. Those eight categories, in my opinion, help me live a rounded life. If any category doesn't resonate with you, feel free to substitute with one of your own.

Week 8: Take Action to Achieve Your Goals

Now that you have set goals, create action tasks for each of those goals. If money and finance is your top priority, then place importance on this one, then move on to other goals. Use the "Create Tasks for Your Savings Goal Worksheet" and the "How Much Money Do You Actually Need to Live Your Dream Life Worksheet" to complete this task. This will become your non-negotiable goal for the next week or two.

Take baby steps and keep doing the amazing work, day after day, week after week. Once momentum is built and a tipping point is reached, amazing things will start happening–things that you never thought would change in your life.

Acknowledgments

I want to thank my family, near and far, for their support and input for this book.

This book would not be possible without all my life lessons. I thank all the teachers in my life who enabled me to explore life as it is meant to be. Some people came and left this earth early, but nevertheless introduced me to key concepts including spirituality. Thank you, Mihir Thaker and Belinda Harber.

I want to thank all the amazing women who spent their valuable time sharing their stories with me. Thank you Bianca Hartge-Hazelman, Bronwyn Reid, Christa Malkin, Helen Robinett, Dr.Jillian Kenny, Kate Christie, Leanne Blaney, Leonara Risse, Nicola Barnard, Sadhana Smiles, and Susan Bryant.

I would also like to thank the team behind getting this book out—from editing to graphics design to cover to the layout of the book to printing. Thank you for making my dream come true. I hope I have not missed anyone; but if I have, it is not intentional.

Finally, a big thank you to my readers. I would love to hear from you about anything that has inspired you: you can write to me at obu.ramaraj@ smartmoneysolutions.com.au.

About the Author

Obu Ramaraj is the managing director of Smart Money Solutions and helps women take control of their financial lives, so they can grow their savings. After spending nearly a decade in the financial industry, Obu knows what is truly important to plan and achieve the desired lifestyle for women—and it's not just about making more and more money. It is about being conscious of your thoughts about money!

Obu's experience is quite unique in that she is a first-generation Australian Indian and worked as a research scientist in her previous life. She has now built a six-figure business from the ground up in finance while raising two young kids and acting as chief financial officer at home. She is also the author of *Smart Women, Smart Home Loans,* a guide to help homebuyers with their home loans.

Obu has been nominated for various awards, like the Telstra Business Women's Award, the AusMumprenuer Award, and has been a finalist in the Wyndham Business Awards and the Indian Executive Club Awards.

Obu has landed coverage in print and radio around the world, including the *Huffington Post,* Westpac's *Ruby Connection*, and Southern FM. Her own articles have been featured in *Australian Financial Review, Women's Agenda, The Indian Sun, Working Women,* and *Women's Business Society.*

Obu is the founder and former president of Inner Wheel Club of Point Cook (a nonprofit, international, women's organization) and has been on the board of two nonprofit organizations. She loves music and is being trained to play an old Indian classical instrument, called "veena."

Connect with Me

Twitter – twitter.com/smartloanbroker

Facebook – www.facebook.com/oburamaraj

Email – Obu.ramaraj@smartmoneysolutions.com.au

Blog/website – www.oburamaraj.com